The Republican Civil War

THE REPUBLICAN CIVIL WAR

WHAT LIZ CHENEY'S WYOMING
TELLS US ABOUT A DIVIDED
AMERICAN RIGHT

STEPHANIE MURAVCHIK
AND
JON A. SHIELDS

OXFORD
UNIVERSITY PRESS

OXFORD
UNIVERSITY PRESS

Oxford University Press is a department of the University of Oxford.
It furthers the University's objective of excellence in research, scholarship,
and education by publishing worldwide. Oxford is a registered trade mark of
Oxford University Press in the UK and in certain other countries.

Published in the United States of America by Oxford University Press
198 Madison Avenue, New York, NY 10016, United States of America.

Library of Congress Cataloging-in-Publication Data
Names: Muravchik, Stephanie, 1970- author | Shields, Jon A. author
Title: The Republican civil war : what Liz Cheney's Wyoming tells us about
a divided American right / Stephanie Muravchik, Jon A. Shields.
Description: New York, NY : Oxford University Press, 2026. |
Series: Studies in postwar American political development |
Includes bibliographical references and index.
Identifiers: LCCN 2025047109 (print) | LCCN 2025047110 (ebook) |
ISBN 9780197832233 paperback | ISBN 9780197832226 hardback |
ISBN 9780197832240 epub | ISBN 9780197832264
Subjects: LCSH: Cheney, Liz, 1966- | Republican Party (Wyo.) |
Republican Party (U.S. : 1854-) | Intra-party disagreements
(Political parties)—Wyoming | Right and left (Political science)—Wyoming |
Wyoming—Politics and government—21st century
Classification: LCC JK2358.W9 M87 2026 (print) | LCC JK2358.W9 (ebook)
LC record available at https://lccn.loc.gov/2025047109
LC ebook record available at https://lccn.loc.gov/2025047110

DOI: 10.1093/oso/9780197832226.001.0001

Paperback printed by Marquis Book Printing, Canada

The manufacturer's authorized representative in the EU for product safety is
Oxford University Press España S.A. of Parque Empresarial San Fernando de Henares,
Avenida de Castilla, 2 – 28830 Madrid (www.oup.es/en or product.safety@oup.com).
OUP España S.A. also acts as importer into Spain of products made by the manufacturer.

To Our Mentors

Brian Balogh and Peter Skerry

CONTENTS

LIST OF FIGURES

LIST OF TABLES

INTRODUCTION

WYOMING MAY SEEM LIKE AN unlikely place for a Republican civil war. No state has been more loyal to Donald Trump than the cowboy state. Nearly 70 percent of Wyomingites voted for Trump in 2016 and 2020, outpacing even deep red North Dakota, Oklahoma, and West Virginia (see Table I.1). Nor has loyalty to Trump softened since the January 6th insurrection. The chair of the Wyoming Republican Party was caught on the Capitol grounds with a walkie-talkie on the 6th. A year later, Liz Cheney was primaried for her outspoken condemnation of Trump, winning just 29 percent of the vote.[1] Now with Cheney vanquished, it seems that if any party can claim to be firmly behind Trump and the party's populist turn, surely it is the Wyoming GOP.

Appearances can be deceiving. After our first Wyoming trip in 2021 to study Cheney's primary race, we stumbled upon something we didn't expect: a fierce factional war that was far older and broader than disputes over Trump's character or rigged national elections. It pivoted around a different fault line: one that divided those who were oriented toward governing from those obsessed with identity. To our surprise, we also found a Republican establishment that hadn't been vanquished. It

---

[1] A recent poll found that 68 percent of Wyoming voters plan to vote for Trump in 2024, roughly the same level of support he won in 2016 and 2020. "Wyoming 2024 Poll," Emerson College Polling, October 17, 2023, https://emersoncollegepolling. com/wyoming-2024-poll-president-biden-with-13-approval-among-wyoming-residents/.

Table I.1 Ten Most Pro-Trump States: Share of Vote for
Republican Presidential Candidate, 2016 and 2020

	2016		2020
Wyoming	68.2%	Wyoming	69.9%
West Virginia	67.9%	West Virginia	68.6%
Oklahoma	65.3%	Oklahoma	65.4%
North Dakota	63.0%	North Dakota	65.1%
Kentucky	62.5%	Idaho	63.8%
Alabama	62.1%	Arkansas	62.4%
South Dakota	61.5%	Kentucky	62.1%
Tennessee	60.7%	Alabama	62.0%
Arkansas	60.6%	South Dakota	61.8%
Idaho	59.2%	Tennessee	60.7%

Sources: New York Times, "2016 Presidential Election Results," August 9, 2017, https://www.nytimes.com/elections/2016/results/president; CNN, "Presidential Results," 2020, https://www.cnn.com/election/2020/results/president.

was more powerful and resilient than we anticipated. In fact, it was still in control of the state legislature, albeit barely—and fighting with some success to regain lost ground in the state party.

This book is an effort to understand this civil war by interviewing and observing the elected officials and activists on its front lines. We traveled all across Wyoming, from Sheridan in the north to Cheyenne in the south, from Wheatland in the east to Evanston in the west, interviewing local political activists, candidates, consultants, and elected officials. We also observed politics up close by attending state conventions, fundraisers, small candidate meet-and-greets, and the like.

It wasn't easy. The state of Wyoming is a challenging place to do interviews and observe politics. Roughly half of its population lives in communities with 10,000 residents or fewer, and they are separated by vast stretches of empty plains. That means that one can drive all day to do a single interview. Those who have campaigned in the state, the Cheneys included, know these challenges well. Mary Cheney, Dick's youngest daughter, recalled them as she tagged along on her father's House election campaigns: "My dad once drove three hours from Casper to Laramie to have coffee with three voters."[2] We, too, drove long distances, sometimes just to interview a single activist or politician. (For interested readers, we have tucked a fuller description of our method in the Appendix.)

The Republican civil war has gone mostly unnoticed in deep red states like Wyoming partly because political scientists have largely neglected doing careful, in-depth studies of state-level politics.[3] And in those rare cases where such work has been done—like Kathy Cramer's study of Wisconsin politics and Ken Miller's study of Texas and California—it has focused on left–right conflicts rather than intra-partisan ones.[4] To our knowledge, there is no major study of intra-party conflict in any American state.[5] Meanwhile, as local journalism has withered, we have even less knowledge of state-level politics than we once did.[6] That's an oversight since most of the contests over political power play out locally—in battles over county parties, state senate races, and other local offices. The fate of the Republican Party will be shaped

---

[2] Mary Cheney, *Now It's My Turn: A Daughter's Chronicle of Political Life* (Threshold Editions, 2006), 18.

[3] Most work on intra-party conflict focuses on national politics. See, for example, Ruth Bloch Rubin, *Building the Bloc: Intraparty Organization in the US Congress* (Cambridge University Press, 2017); Rachel M. Blum and Mike Cowburn, "How Local Factions Pressure Parties: Activist Groups and Primary Contests in the Tea Party Era," *British Journal of Political Science* 54, no. 1 (2024): 88–109; Andrew J. Clarke, "Party Sub-Brands and American Party Politics," *American Journal of Political Science* 64, no. 3 (2020): 452–70.

[4] Katherine J. Cramer, *The Politics of Resentment: Rural Consciousness in Wisconsin and the Rise of Scott Walker* (University of Chicago Press, 2016); Kenneth P. Miller, *Texas vs. California: A History of Their Struggle for the Future of America* (Oxford University Press, 2020). The neglect of state-level politics is a long-standing one. See Malcolm E. Jewell, "The Neglected World of State Politics," *Journal of Politics* 44, no. 3 (1982): 638–57.

[5] The closest is Rachel Blum's excellent book on the insurgent strategies of Tea Party activists in Ohio and Virginia. However, it neglects counter-mobilization on the part of establishment Republicans, and it doesn't fully explicate the deeper ideational divide that lies at the heart of this civil war. See Rachel M. Blum, *How the Tea Party Captured the GOP: Insurgent Factions in American Politics* (University of Chicago Press, 2020).

[6] Margaret Sullivan, *Ghosting the News: Local Journalism and the Crisis of American Democracy* (Columbia Global Reports, 2020).

by thousands of these skirmishes, not just battles over higher-profile federal offices.

To see the Republican civil war most nakedly, it also helps to study it in a one-party state like Wyoming. Like so many other American polities and institutions, Wyoming has become more politically homogeneous in recent decades. While a bit fewer than half of all voters registered as Republicans in 1972, roughly 80 percent did so in 2024. That has made it a far less hospitable place for Democrats to win elections.[7] Currently, Wyoming has only seven elected Democrats in its statehouse, leaving it with the lowest overall percentage of any state legislature in the nation (Table I.2). Without many Democrats about, essentially all politics in Wyoming now pivots around factional conflicts within the Republican Party. It consumes local activists and politicians. This is why, after a Trump speech in Casper, Wyoming, his remarks were understood in the local context of factional Republican feuds. Elizabeth "Biffy" Jackson, then the chair of the Uinta County

Table I.2 Share of Democratic Legislators in Republican-Controlled State Legislatures, 2024

Wyoming	7.5%
West Virginia	10.4%
South Dakota	10.5%
North Dakota	11.3%
Idaho	17.1%
Arkansas	17.7%
Oklahoma	18.8%

Source: National Conference of State Legislatures, "2024 State & Legislative Partisan Composition," April 29, 2024, https://documents.ncsl.org/wwwncsl/About-State-Legislatures/Legis_Control_2024_5.18.24_02.pdf.

---

7 However, Wyoming has always been a Republican state. See James D. King et al., *The Equality State: Government and Politics in Wyoming* (Macmillan, 2017), 27–30; State of Wyoming, "Statewide Summary: Wyoming Voter Registration," January 2024, https://sos.wyo.gov/Elections/Docs/VRStats/2024/24JanVR_Stats.pdf.

Republican Party, noted that the former president said "one thing" that "really resonated." "He said we don't need to worry about them Democrats." Instead, Jackson said, "the real threat comes from within."[8]

The revival of intra-party conflict—long the norm in American politics—is itself fueled by partisan polarization.[9] As states, cities, and the professions become more like the state of Wyoming—ideologically uniform and socially isolated—internecine conflicts are starting to fracture them. This is partly because group homogeneity creates an opportunity for activists and candidates to seek power by making ever more strident, quasi-religious demands. On the left, we see these family feuds play out in progressive cities and universities over issues ranging from policing to free speech to the Israel–Hamas war in Gaza. On the right, as we'll see, conservative infighting looks different in some respects. These feuds are less driven by policy differences and they have been less visible, too, largely because they take place in rural communities far removed from media centers and public attention. But on both the right and the left we also see a common pattern: New insurgent activists and politicians, driven by nationalized movements and distrustful of their respective establishments, are pushing various forms of identity politics.

These new campaigns advance further in one-party places—whether they are blue cities like Portland, far-left campuses like Oberlin College, or far-right red states like Wyoming. But precisely because that is so, new insurgencies invite resistance when they inevitably transgress boundaries others consider reasonable and sacred. Too often we simply assume elite acquiescence to the new insurgents, when in fact there is institutional resistance and counter-mobilization. We notice the more demonstrative (and often outrageous) behavior of the insurgents and miss the quieter forms of institutional resistance. For example, even in some of the most "woke" colleges and universities, serious subterranean battles often rage over their mission and curriculum. And despite everything we hear about the MAGA right's takeover of the GOP,

---

[8] Facebook post, Biffy Jackson, May 29, 2022.

[9] Steve Teles and Rob Saldin anticipated this development. See Steven M. Teles and Robert P. Saldin, "The Future Is Faction," *National Affairs* (Fall 2020), https://nationalaffairs.com/publications/detail/the-future-is-faction.

establishment Republicans have not abandoned ship even in uber-red Wyoming. As we'll see, they have been quietly counter-mobilizing by forming organizations, raising money, and recruiting candidates. They have even forged an alliance with the tiny contingent of Democrats in the state legislature.

Establishments—both right and left—do confront a serious disadvantage, though. Their enemies find it easier to mobilize the moral passions of their followers, while members of aged establishments more easily become wearied by conflict and are tempted to retreat from battle. It is always hard to match the zeal of quasi-religious believers, looking to transform their political and professional institutions into little holy lands. That zeal may also be easier to sustain in an age in which more Americans are looking for religious substitutes for the churches they no longer attend. As we'll see, some of the most committed activists migrated to Wyoming from blue states, looking for a conservative mecca—a refuge in a nation gone "woke." In this way, too, polarization fuels Wyoming's Republican civil war.

This doesn't mean that there isn't a constituency for the establishment either in Wyoming or elsewhere. A recent study that drew on American National Election Survey data found that intra-party divisions are developing in the electorate, with moderate Democrats and Republicans cooling on their respective parties. As the authors conclude: "Despite partisan and ideological sorting, parties are becoming internally divided. Stronger ideological identifiers continue to express very positive feelings toward their party, but ideologically moderate partisans like their party less." They further assume that the moderates "have nowhere to sort."[10] But that is less obviously so in more local, one-party settings like Wyoming. The irony may be, then, that such places may be the incubators of organized resistance against the excesses of American polarization.

These developments were anticipated by the American Founders. They understood that small, homogenous republics would provide no relief from the "mischiefs of faction." "So strong is this propensity of mankind to fall into mutual animosities," James Madison observed,

---

[10] Eric Groenendyk et al., "*Intra*party Polarization in American Politics," *Journal of Politics* 82, no. 4 (2020): 1616–20.

"that where no substantial occasion presents itself, the most frivolous and fanciful distinctions have been sufficient to kindle their unfriendly passions and excite their most violent conflicts."[11] Although Madison may have slighted the seriousness of our moral differences and aspirations, he captured something important about our schismatic nature.

Thus, we should anticipate a political future shaped not merely by partisan polarization but by intense infighting as well. Much recent research has focused on our conformist tendency, our willingness to accept the claims of our tribe.[12] Not enough work has attended to our schismatic tendencies.[13] Our proliferating factional conflicts deserve more scrutiny from political scientists, particularly since such quarrels have historically been a critical engine of political change in American politics.[14] That means not ignoring seemingly homogeneous polities like Wyoming.

And while this is a study about Wyoming, it would be a mistake to assume that the Republican civil war only rages in the cowboy state. In red states—including Texas, Idaho, Nebraska, South Dakota, South Carolina, and Tennessee—Republican elites are at war with populists from the MAGA-verse, fighting for the future of their party. While its ultimate outcome is impossible to see, too many political observers have either prematurely written obituaries for the old party or failed to see any meaningful differences between the old and new guard Republicans.[15]

* * * * *

---

[11] *Federalist*, no. 10.

[12] See, for example, Caitlin O'Conner and James Owen Weatherall, *The Misinformation Age: How False Beliefs Spread* (Yale University Press, 2018); Steve Kornacki, *The Red and the Blue: The 1990s and the Birth of Political Tribalism* (Ecco, 2018); Jonathan Haidt, *The Righteous Mind: Why Good People Are Divided by Politics and Religion* (Vintage, 2013).

[13] One exception is the aforementioned study on intra-party polarization in the electorate.

[14] Daniel DiSalvo, *Engines of Change: Party Factions in American Politics, 1868–2010* (Oxford University Press, 2012).

[15] See, for example, Jacob S. Hacker and Paul Pierson, *Let Them Eat Tweets: How the Right Rules in an Age of Extreme Inequality* (Liveright Publishing, 2020); Nicole Hemmer, *Partisans: The Conservative Revolutionaries Who Remade American Politics in the 1990s* (Basic Books, 2022).

Wyoming's Republican civil war isn't a conflict over ideology. It doesn't pit social conservatives against libertarians. Wyoming Republicans generally agree on the issues: They oppose abortion, champion gun rights, and prefer low taxes.

That local consensus is generally shared by the party outside of Wyoming as well. Even the party's most bitter rivalries—like the one between Liz Cheney and Trump—have little to do with policy differences. During Cheney's first two terms as Wyoming's lone representative, she voted with Trump 93 percent of the time, more often than Elise Stefanik (who replaced Cheney as conference chair) and nearly as often as then minority leader Kevin McCarthy.[16] Cheney is no Republican in name only (RINO) or Rockefeller Republican.

This consensus has been hard won. In the 1950s and 1960s Republicans were sharply divided between centrists and conservatives, a clash that culminated in the 1964 primary race between Nelson Rockefeller and Barry Goldwater. Since that time, these divisions have gradually weakened as Americans sorted themselves along ideological lines. Conservative Democrats became Republicans and liberal Republicans became Democrats, leaving both parties much more ideologically homogeneous. Today party polarization is much worse as a consequence, affecting life far beyond the beltway.

By the 1990s, though, Republicans were comparatively more united around ideology than Democrats, who were often divided over the competing priorities of the various social groups they represent. As Matt Grossman and David Hopkins observed in *Asymmetric Politics*, the relative ideological cohesion of Republicans encouraged them to "prize demonstrations of ideological purity and to pressure their party leaders to reject moderation and compromise."[17]

The desire for purity and symbolic victories bred by ideological agreement, though, has opened a political chasm more profound than ideology. Wyoming's Republican civil war runs far deeper. It even runs

---

[16] Jack Brewster, "Who's More Loyal?: Cheney Voted with Trump More Than Possible Replacement Stefanik," *Forbes*, May 6, 2021, https://www.forbes.com/sites/jackbrewster/2021/05/06/whos-more-loyal-cheney-voted-more-with-trump-than-possible-successor-stefanik/?sh=1b67c65d32e1.

[17] Matt Grossman and David A. Hopkins, *Asymmetric Politics: Ideological Republicans and Group Interest Democrats* (Oxford University Press, 2016), 23.

deeper than a disagreement over which issues to prioritize, as some scholars have contended.[18] That's because the Republican civil war is fundamentally a disagreement about the very nature of politics. That is, Republicans in both camps have a fundamentally different sense of what politics is. They disagree about its purpose and meaning.

On one side are governing conservatives, which we will refer to variously throughout the book as the "old guard," "old heads," the "old line," and the "establishment." This type once dominated state politics. For these conservatives, politics is about finding policy remedies to everyday, *local* challenges and problems, like how to distribute a limited number of liquor licenses, fix the state's tax structure, and fund its public schools. This governance-oriented philosophy, of course, is shaped by the conservative orientation of Wyoming's political class and its economic interests. But it is also softened by pragmatic considerations and a larger sense of noblesse oblige.

The old guard limited conflict through a number of norms. One was a taboo about bringing national issues of little relevance to day-to-day governance into state politics. In addition, conflict on state and local matters was modulated through strong institutional norms, especially civility and compromise. As a consequence, politics lacked much of the heated contentiousness of states that have more competitive parties. As one admirer of the old party told us, Republican politics was "frankly boring."

Like other "legacy" families in Wyoming, the Cheneys were educated in this older school of politics. Dick Cheney, who served in the House seat Liz Cheney just lost, was famously uncomfortable in the limelight, preferring to work diligently behind the scenes. Resembling other Wyoming politicians of the old school, Dick Cheney frowned on grandstanders—a sensibility that made him dislike his brasher colleagues bent on remaking the party in their image, especially Newt Gingrich.[19] Always a workhorse, Liz Cheney followed her father's example, gaining a reputation in Wyoming for studiously representing

---

[18] Rachel Blum, for example, argues that the new conservatives seek to "prioritize a different package of issue positions, oriented around the perception of threat," including immigration and guns. See Blum, *How the Tea Party Captured the GOP*, 76.

[19] Stephen F. Hayes, *Cheney: The Untold Story of America's Most Powerful and Controversial Vice President* (HarperCollins, 2007), 3, 6, 147, 160, 505–6.

the state's interests. In these ways, the Cheneys exemplified Wyoming's Republican establishment: They were hard-working legislators, without flash or self-aggrandizement.

Then, as the Tea Party gained momentum, a new model of representative began to make its mark in Wyoming politics. For these new insurgents, politics is less about ordinary governance and policymaking than it is about expressing and affirming their identities as true conservatives. That is the primary end of politics.

While the new conservative politics that is polarizing Wyoming's GOP is all about identity, it seems less anchored to racial identity than some scholars might predict.[20] Yes, prejudiced views of non-whites are certainly common enough in places like Wyoming. As Nicholas Jacobs and Daniel Shea note in *The Rural Voter*, "there is no escaping prejudicial and stereotypical beliefs about racial minorities." Even so, they don't seem to drive Wyoming's Republican civil war.[21] After all, practically all Wyoming Republicans agree that critical race theory should not reshape public school curriculums in the state. Few are fans of mass immigration. And some of the most zealous practitioners of the new identity politics who have been elected to the state legislature are nonwhite. In fact, the only Black female currently elected to the Wyoming legislature is Lynn Hutchings, a new right firebrand. This does not seem to be an intra-partisan war over race, at least not primarily.

For Wyoming's identitarian right, expressions of authentic conservatism rest primarily on four social constructs: 1) rural consciousness, 2) working-class identity, 3) creedalism, and 4) national conservatism.

---

[20] A substantial body of research has attributed Trump's rise to racial resentment. See, for example, Alan I. Abramowitz, *The Great Alignment: Race Party Transformation, and the Rise of Donald Trump* (Yale University Press, 2018); John Sides et al., *Identity Crisis: The 2016 Campaign and the Battle for the Meaning of America* (Princeton University Press, 2018). That work, though, has been challenged by other research. See, for instance, Ben Enke, "Moral Values and Voting: Trump and Beyond," NBER Working Paper 24268 (National Bureau of Economic Research, January 2018), https://www.nber.org/system/files/working_papers/w24268/revisions/w24268.revo.pdf; Benjamin Enke, "Moral Values and Voting," *Journal of Political Economy* 128, no. 10 (2020): 3679–729; Stephanie Muravchik and Jon A. Shields, *Trump's Democrats* (Brookings Institution Press, 2020).

[21] Nicholas F. Jacobs and Daniel M. Shea, *The Rural Voter: The Politics of Place and the Disuniting of America* (Columbia University Press, 2023), 18.

First, conservative identity in Wyoming is attached to the state's vast frontier (Chapter 1). Truly authentic conservatives are understood to hail from the most rural parts, not the state's two largest cities (Casper and Cheyenne). In those dusty, less forgiving places, citizens must hunt, work the land, and manage without the comforts of city life.

The rural–urban divide is among the oldest in American politics. And it remains an important source of political division. Political scientists have found that rural Americans feel both culturally distinct and neglected by urban elites—and that those resentments are an important source of right-wing populism.[22] Our work, though, shows that rural identity doesn't just drive a wedge between the denizens of the red countryside and neighboring blue cities. It also fuels the Republican civil war in Wyoming. Conservative identitarians in Wyoming distrust the state's two most urbanized counties (Natrona and Laramie), regarding them as the home of the Republican establishment. Hence, they successfully stripped these counties of nearly all of their state delegates. And currently new right Republicans are insisting that districts in the state legislature should be drawn along county lines. While the change would be in violation of the one-person, one-vote constitutional requirement, it would certainly give more voice to sparsely populated places.

The new right's effort to purge delegates and remake legislative districts rests partly on the assumption that procedural fairness doesn't always lead to substantive justice for those who have been marginalized from power. In this way, the new right echoes progressive pleas for racial equity. Just as the new left claims that *race-blind* policies are objectionable when they reproduce racial inequality, Wyoming's new right insists that *place-blind* policies are unacceptable when they put rural people at a disadvantage.

Wyoming's insurgent right also tends to define itself against the professional class that has traditionally dominated state politics

---

[22] Cramer, *Politics of Resentment*. See also Nicholas F. Jacobs and B. Kal Minus, "Place-Based Imagery and Voter Evaluations: Experimental Evidence on the Politics of Place," *Political Research Quarterly* 72, no. 2 (2019): 263–77; Robert Wuthnow, *The Left Behind: Decline and Rage in Rural America* (Princeton University Press, 2018); Jacobs and Shea, *Rural Voter*.

(Chapter 2). For the insurgents, class is not understood in narrowly economic terms. As in the rest of America, class has more to do with culture than economics, shaping everything from manners to aesthetics. While the old guard conservatives practice a politics that requires values dear to their social class (like gentility), the new insurgents regard such values as markers of elites' social distance from middle America. Instead, they prize crasser manners and manly shows of strength. This is partly because they, like much of middle America, are more firmly rooted in an honor culture that emphasizes the importance of defending a social reputation for toughness. Hence, gentility and compromise are often read as weakness.

To its credit, the new identity politics has also achieved something we might applaud in our new gilded age: It has allowed citizens from more humble backgrounds to wield political power. Roughly half the new right legislators do not have 4-year college degrees. One Wyomingite was even elected to the state Senate after campaigning for office as he delivered pizzas. And the current chair of the state party once worked as a Terminix inspector, replacing an old guard type who left the state to take a job at Google.

There is also something admittedly democratic about the new identity politics. It doesn't demand any technocratic knowledge, like familiarity with budgets or arcane policy issues.[23] Mostly one just needs to understand what an authentic conservative is and act accordingly. That makes it more accessible to citizens with less formal education.

Much has rightly been made of the new "diploma divide" that is realigning American parties. Whites with college degrees have been drifting into the Democratic Party, while those without them have been embracing the Republican Party.[24] But this book highlights something

---

[23] See Edward Carmines and James Stimpson's distinction between "hard" and "easy" issues. Edward G. Carmines and James A. Stimson, "The Two Faces of Issue Voting," in *Classics in Voting Behavior*, ed. Richard G. Neimi and Herbert F. Weisberg (Congressional Quarterly Press, 1994); also see John McWhorter, *Woke Racism: How a New Religion Has Betrayed Black America* (Portfolio, 2021), 76–79.

[24] See, for example, Matt Grossman and David A. Hopkins, *Divided by Degrees: How the Diploma Divide and the Culture War Transformed American Politics* (Cambridge University Press, 2024); Patrick Ruffini, *Party of the People: Inside the Populist Working Class Coalition Remaking the GOP* (Simon and Schuster, 2023).

that has gone largely unnoticed: This same diploma divide is also remaking the GOP, dividing old and new guard Republicans in a bitter war over the future of their party.

Of course, these intra-party divisions along the lines of class and place both mirror and are nested within social cleavages that are polarizing Democrats and Republicans. As progressivism has become closely associated with college-educated urbanites, it is not so surprising that some of the new conservatives look with suspicion on old guard Republicans from Casper and Cheyenne. Through the eyes of new insurgents, those establishment elites look a bit too like Democrats. In this way, too, national polarization is shaping Wyoming's civil war.

Aside from belonging to a rugged, rural working class, members of the new right are also expected to express an unflinching devotion to a well-defined creed, much like Protestants affirm their devotion to the Apostles' Creed. (Chapter 3). A true conservative cares only about a finite set of sacred causes, ranging from guns to abortion to critical race theory. This is partly why state party platforms matter so much to Wyoming's new right. Hence, politics is not something that bubbles up from shifting human needs and problems but rather is handed down from something akin to political theology. For creedalists, therefore, there is no politics below these finite issues, no larger realm of public need. That world can—and should—be neglected. Instead, a genuine conservative must focus on demonstrating their personal devotion to a set of national causes that matter.

One good way to do that is to exile anyone who doesn't perfectly toe the line. Naming and shaming heretics is now widely practiced in the Wyoming GOP, and it has created a conservative cancel culture as unforgiving as its progressive rival. In this respect, the new conservatism resembles progressive identity politics far more than most observers have appreciated.

Liz Cheney, who was censured twice by the state party, is only the best-known victim of the new conservative cancel culture. Many others have been called out as well for crimes that include support for Medicaid expansion. The new censors have developed websites, like WyoRINO, which help party officials and activists identify heretical Republicans.

The politicians and party officials who are singled out for censure, though, generally have one thing in common: They hail from Wyoming's upper class. They tend to have either advanced degrees or great wealth—and sometimes both. Such class markers make them especially suspect conservatives in a party that is increasingly identified with a rugged working class.

The issues to which members of the new right are expected to express fealty, moreover, tend to be *national* ones, driven by social media and personalities from the MAGA-verse (Chapter 4). Thus, Wyoming's new right has accelerated the nationalization of politics in the state, a trend that is deforming local and state politics everywhere. As Daniel Hopkins has shown, political parties no longer offer their own local brands, at least not to the same extent they once did. Much like our suburban commercial strips, which are crowded with the same national chains, our local political offerings look increasingly alike as well.[25]

From the old guard's point of view, one problem with the nationalization of Wyoming politics is that it distracts the legislature from addressing actual problems that affect Wyomingites. So, while the old guard doesn't like critical race theory, it also doesn't think it's being taught in Wyoming public schools. And that means the issue is a low priority. This is why in primary races against new right candidates, the establishment types stress the need to focus on "real" problems.

But for those of the new right, oriented as they are around establishing their identity as true conservatives devoted to a national creed, it is important to speak out on issues like critical race theory. Doing so integrates them into a national creedal war against the social justice left. And, here again, we see the tendency of national polarization to drive Wyoming's Republican civil war.

Perhaps most surprising, Wyoming's Republican establishment is still alive. It's aggressively counter-mobilizing, even reclaiming some political turf it had lost (Chapter 5). And if the new conservative politics of identity can be held at bay in Wyoming—the most pro-Trump state

---

[25] Daniel J. Hopkins, *The Increasingly United States: How and Why American Political Behavior Nationalized* (University of Chicago Press, 2018).

in the union—then the party Liz Cheney embodied still might have a future.

*****

Few elites have been excoriated more severely than those in the Republican establishment—and from so many quarters. Liberals say that they have failed to defend democracy against Trump's illiberalism. Social democrats say they are merely self-dealing oligarchs. And MAGA-aligned intellectuals insist that they lack the resolve and strength to combat left-wing identity politics. For all their differences, these camps suggest that the problems with the establishment's rule spring from the compromised character of its elites. Old guard Republicans, it seems, are simply too spineless and self-serving. In the Chapter 6, we assess these criticisms. And, to varying degrees, we find them wanting.

The sharpest critics have been those concerned with the future of liberal democracy. They stress that too many politicians in the Republican establishment haven't resisted Trump's democratic norm-breaking.[26] And while we are broadly sympathetic to these thinkers, our time in Wyoming also left us with the sense that they were missing something. Far beyond the beltway, in red states like Wyoming, we found local politicians who were working hard to defend liberal democracy by defending democratic norms. Perhaps because such places are still relatively insulated from Trump's attentive gaze as well as the national media's, old guard Republicans have felt freer to fight the MAGA-fication of their party than their counterparts in the US Congress. In any case, greater attention to state-level politics should provide a fuller account of our somewhat one-dimensional view of the GOP establishment.

A more long-standing criticism of the Republican establishment comes from progressives of a social democratic bent. They have long hoped that the white working class would turn against an allegedly plutocratic party, one controlled by affluent doctors, bankers, and oil magnates. More recently, some intellectuals on the MAGA right have been rooting for the same outcome. Perhaps they should be careful what

---

[26] See, for example, Steven Levitsky and Daniel Ziblatt, *How Democracies Die* (Broadway Books, 2018).

they hope for. The once lowly are toppling the strong in Wyoming. But we suspect that intellectuals on the social democratic left won't like the GOP much if its establishment falls.

That's true in part because these yearnings for revolution rest on a falsehood. While influential books like Thomas Frank's *What's the Matter with Kansas* rightly understand that the GOP is coming apart along lines of social class, they wrongly insist that its party elites were simply plutocratic. In Frank's telling these elites are simply rapacious, consumed with padding their wealth at the expense of the party's working-class voters.[27] Like other myths, Frank's indictment contained a kernel (or two) of truth. The GOP establishment in Wyoming—like its counterparts in other states—was insular, and it succumbed to self-dealing now and then.

But it was always wrong to simply see the Republican establishment as a corrupt plutocracy. Whatever its misdeeds, Wyoming's Republican establishment was also public-spirited. It worked hard and was genuinely concerned about Wyoming's common good. In fact, the same public-spiritedness that Cheney brought to the January 6th Commission is evident in so many members of the establishment. They have long labored away for little compensation in a demanding part-time legislature that meets during Wyoming's frigid winter. And they have redistributed money away from its rich industries toward public goods like education. As a consequence, Wyoming spends more on education than most other states, including many progressive ones.[28] That so many working- and middle-class Americans are now leaving blue states like California to seek jobs and opportunity in red states should also lead us to wonder whether Republican governance more generally has been as exploitative as Frank and his ilk insist.

More than that, though, members of Wyoming's GOP establishment were the custodians of a nobler form of politics. The old guard venerated the statehouse and its civic norms, especially civility and compromise. It

---

[27] Thomas Frank, *What's the Matter with Kansas? How Conservatives Won the Heart of America* (Metropolitan Books, 2004); Hacker and Pierson, *Let Them Eat Tweets.*

[28] Chris Gilligan, "Which States Invest the Most in Their Students?," *U.S. News & World Report*, August 26, 2022, https://www.usnews.com/news/best-states/articles/2022-08-26/which-states-invest-the-most-in-their-students.

also insisted on keeping national issues of little relevance to day-to-day governance in Wyoming off the state agenda.

That world, once seemingly so inviolable, is now endangered. As the new insurgents have chipped away at the old guard's power in the state party and legislature, they have brought their own style of politics with them. One of the new types insisted that there is "way too much dignity around here." All that dignity, after all, can facilitate compromises and encourage politicians to modulate their speech. It's a wellspring of inauthenticity, an enemy of the new identity politics.

Lost in the demands for truer, authentic conservatives is any acknowledgment that public life requires inauthenticity. That's what makes it different from private life. As the sociologist Richard Sennett observed long ago, we remove our public masks in our private life. In those intimate settings we reveal the darker corners of our souls to those we love and trust. But in our public life, we are citizens who must interact with strangers and our political opponents. Thus, we need to regulate those encounters through norms that shield our fellow citizens from our ugly parts, including our self-righteousness, vengeful impulses, and social resentments.[29]

Trump, of course, is the most notorious exemplar of the new politics of authenticity. From the beginning of his presidency, he mocked the expectation that his speech should be "presidential." By transgressing the norms of a more refined professional class, Trump became a hero of the working class.

The virtues of the old privileged establishment are easier to see now that the new identitarians have infiltrated the state legislature. For them, the point of lawmaking is to express their identity as far-right conservatives, not seek remedies to the more pressing problems that concern average citizens. It's a corrupt populism, claiming to speak for "the people" but in truth having little interest in discovering what the people might actually want.

Some MAGA-aligned intellectuals, though, have persuaded themselves that only the new conservatives can end this age of identity politics. According to them, the right needs more fighters from the

---

[29] Richard Sennett, *The Fall of Public Man*, 40th anniv. ed. (W. W. Norton and Company, 2017).

rugged and manly working class to beat back the "woke" left, not well-mannered lawyers from the genteel establishment. But in Wyoming the new conservatives are mainly consumed with practicing an identity politics that mirrors its left-wing counterpart. As we mentioned, they are even pushing a right-wing version of equity by insisting that the most rural areas of the state should have more voting power than the more urbanized ones. Only the old establishment stands in the way of this "woke" conservatism.

Finally, in the Epilogue, we look ahead to the future of the Republican Party. Whether the GOP establishment will ultimately prevail against the new insurgents is hard to say. Even in deep red Wyoming, the old establishment is embattled but hardly dead. But one thing is clear: The new right isn't going anywhere. Like state establishments elsewhere, the Wyoming GOP has become a more broad-based working-class party. The real question, then, is on what terms might old and new guard Republicans coexist?

I

Rural Consciousness

WYOMING SEEMS LIKE THE MOST unlikely state to be home to any discord between city and rural folk. One analysis ranked Wyoming the most rural state in the union, just behind Montana.[1] Its largest city is Cheyenne, population 65,051.[2] That makes it roughly the size of Ohio State University's student population. Casper—the state's second largest city—is a bit smaller, with just under 60,000 residents. "I wouldn't consider it a big metro hub," one member of the old guard told us. The third largest city in Wyoming is Laramie, a small college town that is home to a little over 30,000 citizens.

That means that cultural differences between Wyoming's small cities and their outskirts are much more muted than they are, say, between Minneapolis and the Minnesota countryside. The typical citizen of Casper knows how to ride a horse and shoot a gun, for example. You can hardly walk a mile in Wyoming's two biggest "cities" without running into a gun shop. "There is so much more flattening in Wyoming than

---

[1] Nathaniel Rakich, "How Urban or Rural Is Your State? And What Does That Mean for the 2020 Election," FiveThirtyEight, April 14, 2020, https://fivethirtyeight.com/features/how-urban-or-rural-is-your-state-and-what-does-that-mean-for-the-2020-election/.

[2] US Census Bureau, "Quick Facts: Cheyenne City, Wyoming," https://www.census.gov/quickfacts/fact/table/cheyennecitywyoming/PST045221.

there would be in larger states," a member of the Republican old guard told us. "So, when you get people in here who say, 'no, I'm legitimately from the land' . . . that is baffling to me."

Demonstrations of rural identity are on the rise. Not long ago, few delegates to the annual state convention would have attended with guns strapped to their hips. But many did in 2022. In another departure from old norms, these gun-toting delegates have also taken to wearing their cowboy hats inside the convention center. While wearing cowboy hats is common enough in Wyoming, wearing them indoors is not. "That's not a Wyoming thing," insisted a patron of the old party, mostly because there is no need to wear a cowboy hat indoors. There is, though, if your goal is to sport a costume that signals a conservative social identity. For some, even that costume wasn't quite enough. Joey Correnti, the chair of the Carbon County Republican Party, walked around the convention hall with a custom jacket that read: "Rural Wyoming Matters."

The importance of the new identity politics has not been lost on ambitious opportunists like Harriet Hageman. When Hageman cut a campaign ad in her 2022 primary race against Liz Cheney, for example, she was careful to highlight her rural upbringing rather than the years she spent as a lawyer in Cheyenne. As she strolls through a ranch in cowboy boots, the ad's narrator informs us that Hageman was "raised on a ranch outside of Fort Laramie," a remote Wyoming town with fewer than 300 residents. This upbringing makes her "truly Wyoming," the narrator tells us.[3]

The new right's identity politics is tied to the state's vast frontier. The most authentic conservatives are not from the state's two biggest cities, Cheyenne and Casper. They are from the more dusty, rural parts of the state. In those places, people work the land, hunt, and make do without the comforts of urban life.

These divisions have led to major conflicts within the state party. New right leaders in the state's most rural county parties distrust their rivals from Natrona and Laramie Counties, home to Casper and Cheyenne, respectively. They regard them as the home of Republicans

---

[3] Hageman for Wyoming, "Truly Wyoming," YouTube, 15 sec., https://www.youtube.com/watch?v=MbRVjaGt2xE.

in name only (RINOs) and establishment Republicans more generally. Thus, they successfully purged nearly all of the state delegates
from Natrona and Laramie. Presently, they are laboring to give more
power to rural communities in the state legislature by dividing districts along county lines, thus giving more voice to sparsely populated
places.

These schemes rest partly on the notion that substantive outcomes
matter more than procedural fairness. Since rural areas are neglected,
the new right's reasoning goes, they are entitled to more power. It's a
right-wing version of the more familiar pleas for racial equity on the
left. Just as the left insists that *race-blind* policies are unacceptable if
they lead to unequal outcomes between racial groups, the new right in
Wyoming says that *place-blind* policies won't do if they disadvantage
rural people.

Like Wyoming's class divide, this intra-party conflict both mirrors
and is embedded within a much larger rural–urban divide that is polarizing Democrats and Republicans. As progressivism has become closely
associated with urbanization, it is not so surprising that some Wyomingites look with suspicion on Republicans from Casper and Cheyenne,
particularly since they have vocally opposed the redistribution of political power to the rural counties.

And, of course, rural identities are also closely related to the class-
based ones discussed in the next chapter. Since Wyoming's professional
class is concentrated in Casper and Cheyenne—and is especially represented in the leadership of the respective county parties—it is even
less surprising that the new identitarians see these small cities as the
redoubts of the establishment. Hence, these twin sources of conservative identity—both class and place—tend to reinforce one another in
Wyoming's Republican civil war.

* * * * *

The rural–urban divide is perhaps the oldest in American politics.[4]
At the founding, it drove a wedge between the Anti-Federalists and
the Federalists. While the former defended the agrarian interests of

---

4 See Nicholas F. Jacobs and Daniel Shea, *The Rural Voter: The Politics of Place and
the Disuniting of America* (Columbia University Press, 2023), 61–67.

the sturdy yeomanry, the latter desired an expansive commercial republic anchored in trade and cities. Urbanites around New York City supported the proposed new Constitution, while voters who lived in the countryside tended to oppose it.

In our modern day, this divide has been politicized once again as Republicans have become the party of rural America, while Democrats are firmly anchored in cities. The divide is not just an artifact of the social backgrounds of the people who happen to live in rural and urban places. Even after accounting for differences in income, race, and education, rural and urban Americans still have different political views.[5] Thus, women, racial minorities, and white college graduates who live in a rural community are likely to be more conservative than their urban counterparts.

Rural Americans not only live in a different world than urbanites; they're also more attached to the particular places they call home. These small towns and counties confer a strong sense of belonging and identity, making their citizens reluctant to move far from home even when economic opportunity beckons.[6] David Goodhart has called these localists "somewheres," in contrast to cosmopolitan "anywheres." The latter are the members of the highly mobile professional class.[7]

A broader, rural identity knits these more parochial attachments together, in roughly the same way that the construct "people of color" helps to weave various racial and ethnic groups together into a national political coalition. What they share is a distrust of urbanites and the "anywheres" who live there. And they share a sense of "linked fate" as well. That is, they tend to believe that their own individual fortunes depend on the welfare of the group as a whole.[8] Careful fieldwork by Katherine Cramer in Wisconsin shows that rural Americans feel both

---

[5] James Gimpel et al., "The Urban–Rural Gulf in American Political Behavior," *Political Behavior* 42, no. 4 (2020): 1343–68.

[6] Robert Wuthnow, *Small-Town America: Finding Community, Shaping the Future* (Princeton University Press, 2013); Stephanie Muravchik and Jon A. Shields, *Trump's Democrats* (Brookings Institution Press, 2020), 93–120.

[7] David Goodhart, *The Road to Somewhere: The Populist Revolt and the Future of Politics* (Hurst and Company, 2017).

[8] Jacobs and Shea, *Rural Voter*, 163–64, 185; roughly the same idea is developed in Muravchik and Shields, *Trump's Democrats*, 121–47.

culturally distinct and neglected by urban elites. Collectively, these beliefs give rise to what Cramer calls "rural consciousness."[9]

Rural identity, though, isn't just something that divides the red countryside from blue cities and suburbs. Well before Cheney's crusade against Trump, it fueled the Republican civil war in Wyoming. That surprised us since Wyoming's two "big" cities—Casper and Cheyenne—are hardly metropolises. Even so, there are some real differences between conservatives in the state's two small cities and their hinterlands. While the new insurgents have taken over nearly all the county parties in rural areas, they have struggled to seize either the Natrona or Laramie party, home to Casper and Cheyenne, respectively. This is because these more urbanized parties are still controlled by a large contingent of old guard Republicans, drawn from a larger professional class.

Through Trump's first term, the Natrona party was led by Joe McGinley, a Casper-based doctor and formidable foe of the new insurgents. Under his leadership, the party refused to censor any so-called RINOs, Liz Cheney included. McGinley has also been a fierce critic of the state party chair Frank Eathorne and has even called for his resignation.[10] He has also beaten back efforts by his enemies to take over the Natrona party, largely by recruiting old-fashioned Republicans to run for precinct positions.

Laramie and, especially, Natrona Counties are also home to a disproportionate number of state legislators who are regarded as RINOs by the new insurgents. One site, called "WyoRINO," run by activists who want to purge members of the old guard, ranks all the state's legislators

9 Katherine J. Cramer, *The Politics of Resentment: Rural Consciousness in Wisconsin and the Rise of Scott Walker* (University of Chicago Press, 2016), 5, 9, 10, 12, 40, 59–60, 65, 71, 77, 146. See also Nicholas F. Jacobs and B. Kal Minus, "Place-Based Imagery and Voter Evaluations: Experimental Evidence on the Politics of Place," *Political Research Quarterly* 72, no. 2 (2019): 263–77; Robert Wuthnow, *The Left Behind: Decline and Rage in Rural America* (Princeton University Press, 2018). The divide is evident in other countries as well. See, for example, Davide Luca et al., "Progressive Cities: Urban–Rural Polarisation of Social Values and Economic Development around the World," *Urban Studies* 60, no. 12 (2023): 2329–50; Jacobs and Shea, *Rural Voter*.

10 Victoria Eavis, "Natrona County GOP Asks Wyoming Republican Chairman Eathorne to Resign," *Casper Star-Tribune*, June 21, 2022, https://trib.com/news/state-and-regional/govt-and-politics/natrona-county-gop-asks-wyoming-republican-chairman-eathorne-to-resign/article_0ac0a9e0-f1ac-11ec-995e-2f2e9a31894f.html.

on a scale running from zero (a perfect RINO score) to 100 (a true conservative). The site classifies all politicians who score below a 70 as RINOs. It consistently finds that Natrona and Laramie Counties are overwhelmingly represented by fake conservatives. For example, all four senate districts in Natrona are represented by RINOs. Meanwhile, only two of the county's eight house members pass the bar, and one just barely. One important exception was Chuck Gray, a leader of the new guard who represented the 57th district in Casper for 6 years before being elected secretary of state in 2022.

The rural parts of the state are more mixed. In some rural places, old guard legislators have hung on to their seats, though their grip seems to weaken with each passing election. In others, they are now endangered species. Campbell County, which supported Trump by a wider margin than any other Wyoming county, is now firmly under the control of the new conservatives. Only one of its five state representatives is considered a RINO.

It's in the state party, though, where the new rural identity politics is especially pronounced. After Frank Eathorne took the helm as chair in 2017, rural advocates found a new platform to wage war against the "urban" counties. Eathorne, of course, personified the new identity politics. Eathorne was raised on a small ranch in remote Converse County. And Eathorne is unfailingly in costume as well, always sporting a cowboy hat at party meetings. His predecessors Matt Micheli and Ryan Mulholland—both of the old guard—were of a different sort: Micheli was a Cheyenne-based attorney, while Mulholland made a living in the tech sector. Eathorne ascended to the throne after Mulholland resigned to take a job at Google.[11]

Eathorne, though, has done far more than dress like an authentic Wyomingite. Under his leadership, the state party has tried to redistribute power away from Wyoming's small urban centers. He has attempted to increase the number of rural delegates to the national convention and redraw state legislative districts in ways that enhance the influence of rural counties. And he successfully led a charge to purge

---

[11] Arno Rosenfeld, "Rancher and Former WY Watch Chairman Takes Reins of Wyoming GOP," *Casper Star-Tribune*, September 19, 2017, https://trib.com/news/state-and-regional/govt-and-politics/rancher-and-former-wywatch-chairman-takes-reins-of-wyoming-gop/article_c2f8cac8-78fe-587e-8ea0-5a35e47632d8.html.

Natrona's and Laramie's delegates to the state's annual party convention, thus diminishing the power of the old guard within the party. In the Wyoming GOP, rural conservatives matter more than ever.

But that's not how Eathorne and his ilk see it. In their view, rural voices have been unfairly marginalized within the party for a generation. They point out that state legislative districts once were determined by county boundaries, a scheme that enhanced the power of small communities. In 1960, Wyoming's legislative districts were wildly malapportioned, particularly the Senate. At the time, districts ranged from one senator for about 3,000 residents in rural Teton to one for about 30,000 in Laramie. Overall, about a quarter of Wyoming's population could elect a majority of its senators. The state's lower house was also skewed toward rural counties, though less severely.[12]

Such practices soon ran afoul of the Supreme Court. In the 1960s, a series of cases said that states had to draw their districts so that they were roughly equal in size, according to a "one-person, one-vote" principle. At the time, two-thirds of the nation's state legislatures required that counties or towns be represented in at least one chamber of the statehouse. As was the case in Wyoming, that method privileged rural voters and their interests, resulting in stark inequalities. As political scientists Stephen Ansolabehere and James Snyder put it: "America in the middle of the twentieth century had the most unequal representation of any representative form of government in the world."[13]

Thus, the court intervention resulted in a major redistribution of power in the 1970s. Redrawn districts after the 1970 census had to be guided by the "one-person, one-vote" principle. Public money to rural areas declined. "Had malapportionment continued," estimate Ansolabehere and Snyder, "the overrepresented areas would have received about $7 billion more from the state than they received . . . through the 1970s and 1980s."[14]

---

[12] Sarah Augusta Gorin, "A History and Analysis of Wyoming Legislative Reapportionment Cases, 1963–1991" (master's thesis, University of Wyoming, May 1992), 15.

[13] Stephen Ansolabehere and James M. Snyder Jr., *The End of Inequality: One Person, One Vote and the Transformation of American Politics* (W. W. Norton and Company, 2008), 31, 49.

[14] Ansolabehere and Snyder, *End of Inequality*, 207.

Wyoming tried to comply with the Supreme Court's dictates without jettisoning county-based districts. It did so by simply adding representatives and senators to multi-member districts in Laramie and Natrona. While the scheme reduced disparities, they persisted for decades. Even with its nine representatives in 1990, for example, Laramie County had 8,127 residents for every legislator, far more than most other counties, including Niobrara (2,499), Hot Springs (4,809), and Sublette (4,843). The modal legislative district in 1990 had 6,187 residents for every legislator, considerably fewer than both Laramie and Natrona.[15]

These persistent disparities did not withstand judicial scrutiny. In 1991, a federal district court concluded that Wyoming's districts were unconstitutional, finding that "effective participation by all Wyoming citizens in state government requires that each citizen have an equally effective voice in the election of Wyoming lawmakers."[16] The ruling finally prompted the state to do away with county-based districts, further reducing the power of rural communities.

The issue seemed settled until Frank Eathorne and his ilk revived it in the Trump years. At its 2019 meeting the party's central committee proposed a resolution that "re-enfranchises rural areas" by resurrecting county-based, multi-member legislative districts. The resolution encouraged the state to return to its original Constitution, which in 1890 granted each county two senators. It allowed for more equal representation in the House but only up to a point. While the largest counties would receive more representatives, they would be capped at 10, thereby ensuring a greater rural voice in the lower chamber as well.[17]

Since then, the party's demands have varied somewhat. In 2021 and 2022, for example, it insisted that each county should be represented by one senator, rather than two.[18] That plan would have dramatically decreased the size of the legislature, from 60 to 46 in the House

---

[15] *Gorin v. Karpan*, 775 F. Supp. 1430 (D. Wyo. 1991), 1448.

[16] *Gorin v. Karpan*, 1444–45.

[17] Wyoming Republican Party, "Resolutions Passed by the Wyoming Republican Party Central Committee since State Convention May 2018," https://www.wyoming.gop/_files/ugd/d8b5a1_b2dcca034b6948b3aacec5ee11222349.pdf.

[18] Wyoming Republican Party, "Each Wyoming County Should Be Represented by 1 Senator," passed May 7, 2022, https://www.wyoming.gop/post/each-wyoming-county-should-be-represented-by-1-senator.

and from 30 to 23 in the Senate. Wyoming's House has not been that small since 1903.[19] As its proposals for reform have evolved, though, Wyoming's new right has never wavered from the view that representation in the statehouse should weigh rural areas more heavily than urban ones.

Consistent with this position, the new insurgents often insist that America is a republic, not a democracy. The party's resolution calling for county-based districts says they are based on a "Republican form of government," a phrase repeated three times. To the new insurgents the logic seems straightforward: Just as the American Constitution provides for the equal representation of states in the US Senate, so too should Wyoming have equal representation of counties in its senate. And just as the national government prioritizes rural voices, so, too, should Wyoming.

Such proposals—which have been a staple of the party since Eathorne became chair—rest on two other claims. The first is that rural Wyomingites are a distinct group of people, with their own interests and values. And it's this group, not individuals, that should be represented. This is why a 2022 party resolution of the central committee concluded: "The 'one person one vote' principle goes against those specific principles of representation of groups of people."[20] The second claim says that Wyoming's rural citizens don't have enough power under a one-person, one-vote principle. Following the "one-person, one-vote" principle, the party says, has resulted in "the loss of the representation and understanding of the distinct and unique problems of large areas of the State." This is why the party insists that only a return to the old system would "re-enfranchise" rural counties.[21] And it's why Joey Correnti, the chair of the Carbon County GOP, walks about the

[19] Nick Reynolds, "Wyoming GOP Weighs Plan to Shrink, Reallocate Legislature," WyoFile, July 16, 2021, https://wyofile.com/wyoming-gop-weighs-plan-to-shrink-reallocate-legislature/.

[20] Wyoming Republican Party, "Redistricting in Wyoming," passed January 22, 2022, https://www.wyoming.gop/post/redistricting-in-wyoming.

[21] Wyoming Republican Party, "Resolutions Passed by the Wyoming Republican Party Central Committee since State Convention May 2018," https://www.wyoming.gop/_files/ugd/d8b5a1_b2dcca034b6948b3aacec5ee11222349.pdf.

state convention with a jacket that says "Rural Wyoming Matters," as if countryfolk constitute an insular minority in the state of Wyoming.

These arguments echo progressive calls for racial equity rather than racial equality. Modern-day anti-racists insist that a color-blind system only appears fair on the surface. But in practice it's not since it distributes resources in unequal ways between racial groups. Similarly, Wyoming's new conservatives are insisting that the state's place-blind political system only seems fair on the surface. And since Wyoming's most urbanized communities are doing better than its rural ones, something is wrong with the system. What is needed in both cases, say anti-racists and conservatives, is a system that privileges disadvantaged groups. That is what will balance the scales.

The conservative argument for equity isn't exactly new. When the issue of malapportionment was litigated in the 1960s, rural interests made equity-based appeals to defend the old system. In their study of the conflict, political scientists Stephen Ansolabehere and James Snyder found that defenders of rural privilege argued that "unequal population districts . . . were needed to make political power equal."[22] Only malapportionment, the logic went, would bring about more equal outcomes.

These arguments are being revived in other states as well. In deep red Nebraska, for example, new right legislators are seeking the creation of a state senate which would have three counties in every district.[23] (Nebraska is the only state with a unicameral legislature.) Sponsored by representative Steve Erdman, the proposal is motivated by a desire to enhance rural power as the state population has become more concentrated in Omaha. "My district and many other rural districts," Erdman noted, "feel like they're being left out."[24] And in nearby, far-right Idaho, the state party central committee is calling for the same representative scheme by appealing to the "Republican form of

---

[22] Ansolabehere and Snyder, *End of Inequality*, 58, 191.

[23] "Proposal Would Return Nebraska to Two-House Legislature," *Unicameral Update*, March 10, 2023, https://update.legislature.ne.gov/?p=33765.

[24] Nebraska Legislature, "Transcript Prepared by Clerk of the Legislature Transcribers Office Executive Board March 9, 2023," https://www.nebraskalegislature.gov/FloorDocs/108/PDF/Transcripts/ExecBoard/2023-03-09.pdf.

government" adopted by the Founders.[25] Meanwhile, in 2023, a North Carolina state representative pushed a bill that would have combined counties into pairs, each with one state senator. Like his counterparts in Wyoming, North Carolina's representative offered this argument against the current place-blind system: "Colorado is run by Denver. . . . New Mexico is run by Albuquerque. . . . Chicago runs Illinois."[26] The Texas GOP, which has been at war with establishment Republicans in the state legislature, has gone further than these states: It's advocating for all statewide offices to be elected through a scheme that would shift electoral power dramatically to rural counties. Much like the Electoral College, candidates would need to win the popular vote in a majority of Texas' counties to win statewide office.[27] Not only would the change make it impossible for Democrats to win statewide office; it would also empower new guard Republicans. Elsewhere, Republicans seek the formation of new, more rural states to weaken urban power in their home states. In California, Republicans in its far-north rural counties have hatched a plan to secede, forming a new state with some rural counties in Oregon.[28]

* * * * *

While the Wyoming GOP's plan to return to county-based districts was always quixotic given so many legal and political obstacles, other methods of weakening the power of Natrona and Laramie hold more promise. Thus, the party leadership went to work strengthening the power of rural communities within the state GOP. In the past, for instance, rural counties were not guaranteed a delegate at the national

[25] Idaho Republican Party, "Accepted Resolutions Idaho Republican State Central Committee Meeting," May 8, 2021, 22–23.

[26] Steve Doyle, "Bill Proposes Dividing North Carolina into 50 Two-County Districts with One State Senator Each Regardless of Population," *Fox 8*, March 24, 2023, https://myfox8.com/news/politics/your-local-election-hq/redistricting/bill-proposes-dividing-north-carolina-into-50-two-county-districts-with-one-state-senator-each-regardless-of-population/.

[27] James Bickerton, "Texas GOP Amendment Would Stop Democrats Winning Any State Election," *Newsweek*, May 27, 2024, https://www.newsweek.com/texas-gop-amendment-would-stop-democrats-winning-any-state-election-1904988.

[28] Shawn Hubler, "The State of California's 'State of Jefferson,'" *New York Times*, May 26, 2021, https://www.nytimes.com/2021/05/26/us/california-jefferson-secession.html.

convention, though Laramie—Wyoming's most populous county—
always got one.[29] Finding this inequity unacceptable, the party's central committee recently passed new bylaws that guarantee each county
one delegate at the national convention.[30]

The change outraged party activists in the larger counties. Dani
Olsen, the chair of the Laramie County GOP, lamented that the new
system is less representative. She noted: "Larger population bases like
Laramie County are going to be limited to one vote for the 22,000-plus
registered Republicans and Niobrara County gets one vote for the 1200
registered Republicans they might have." Olsen understands that many
of the party activists from rural counties simply don't see those from
Cheyenne as authentic conservatives. Hence, they are looked upon with
suspicion. "[S]ome counties," she added, "view Laramie County Republicans as 'too moderate,' because of the fact we have more diversity, that
we're not 'Republican enough.'"[31]

More boldly, party officials have also been busy purging whole del-
egations from the Natrona and Laramie County parties—home to
nearly one-third of the state's population. In 2022, for example, nearly
all of Laramie's delegates filed out of the state convention hall in protest
after being stripped of their voting rights, as others whooped and
cheered their exile. One angry Laramie delegate slammed his credential
on the dais as he exited the convention.[32] Eathorne, a prime archi-
tect of the new identity politics, coolly and silently observed the crude

[29] Nick Reynolds, "GOP Official Says Change to Delegate Selection Process
Would Give Outsize Influence to Wyoming's Small Counties," WyoFile, July 17,
2019, https://trib.com/news/state-and-regional/govt-and-politics/gop-official-says-
change-to-delegate-selection-process-would-give/article_92feebae-81c2-5a68-bd1d-
78ab23296eof.html.
[30] Wyoming Republican Party, Bylaws of the Wyoming Republican Party 2022 as
adopted at the Wyoming Republican Party State Convention, May 7, 2022 (Wyoming
Republican Party), 20, https://sos.wyo.gov/Elections/Docs/Wyoming_Republican_
Party_Bylaws_2022.pdf.
[31] Reynolds, "GOP Official Says Change."
[32] Leo Wolfson, "Laramie County Delegates Walk Out of GOP Convention After State Party Vote to Expel," Cowboy State Daily, May 7, 2022, https://
cowboystatedaily.com/2022/05/07/entire-laramie-county-delegation-walks-out-of-
gop-convention-after-state-party-vote-to-expel/; also see Victoria Eavis, "Laramie
County Delegates Walk Out After Losing Delegates at GOP Convention," Casper
Star-Tribune, May 7, 2022, https://trib.com/news/state-and-regional/govt-and-
politics/watch-now-laramie-county-republicans-walk-out-after-losing-delegates-at-

jubilation over the delegation's departure until Scott Clem, a former legislator and Baptist minister, shushed the crowd.

Laramie's crime? The county party neglected to conduct a secret ballot when they selected their delegates for the state convention, a violation of bylaws that probably had little to no substantive effect on the composition of its delegation. Red-faced and teary, Laramie's chair struggled to maintain her composure as she chatted with local media after the purge. Natrona County also only had a handful of delegates at the convention, having been stripped of most of them a year earlier because it refused to pay its own dues in recent years as its leadership battled with powerful hardliners in the state party.[33]

Old guard members say the purges were motivated by rural resentment. Gail Symons, an establishment leader from small Sheridan County, watched in disgust as Laramie delegates marched out of the convention. "It was 'Us small counties' against those leftists in large Laramie County," she told us. "There is this resentment from the smaller counties toward the larger counties that has really been the [cause] of this." Nathan Winters, a state legislator and leader in the Laramie County GOP, agrees with Symons and believes that conservatism should not rest on a place-based identity politics. Rightly understood, "conservatism isn't based on geography," he said. "It's based on principles." But for some party people in rural counties, he lamented, it seems "purely" rooted in geography.

Other old guard Republicans see a more sinister authoritarianism at work. Barbara Cubin—Wyoming's first female elected to the US Congress—likened the purges to Soviet governance. "The behavior is that of the Soviet Politburo," she wrote in a letter to the new party leaders. "In this country, we allow the voice of the opposition."[34]

---

gop-convention/article_4de493b0-ce31-11ec-a3c5-6b7f2d93c1fa.html#tracking-source=most-popular-homepage.

[33] Victoria Eavis, "State GOP Slashes Natrona County Party's Delegate Count," *Casper Star-Tribune*, January 22, 2022.

[34] Nick Reynolds, "GOP Infighting Culminates in Attempt to Block Natrona County from State Convention," *Casper Star-Tribune*, May 9, 2020, https://trib.com/news/state-and-regional/govt-and-politics/gop-infighting-culminates-in-attempt-to-block-natrona-county-from-state-convention/article_a22137c16-1cb9-5f22-a5f9-45a53dd511ee.html.

The result of these purges was a far smaller, purified state convention in 2022, dominated by party activists from the state's most rural counties. "They're trying to consolidate their control of the party," McGinley told us. "The crowd was half the size of the last convention." John Brown, a party activist from Fremont County, has noticed the changes as well: "We used to have 400 delegates plus at the Wyoming GOP state convention—400-plus." "We had just 285 this time," he added. "They're shrinking the voice of the majority." It's a strange kind of populism that shrinks the party.

Even without the purges, the governing structure of the party also ensures a strong rural voice for another reason: The state party's central committee is composed of three representatives from every county party. Thus, large counties like Laramie, with its population of about 100,000, have the same voice in the central committee as small counties like Sublette County, which has fewer than 9,000 residents. That means that, collectively, delegates from Laramie and Natrona make up about 8 percent of the central committee's membership even though those same counties are home to nearly one-third of the state's population.[35]

The power of the central committee, it should be added, is not inconsequential. A major reason Frank Eathorne ascended to become the head of the state party, despite a checkered past, is that the central committee gives so much power to rural activists. As Gail Symons told us, Eathorne and his allies consolidated control of the state party thanks to the support of "about 15 to 16 very small counties." The central committee also has the power to select elected officials, at least on occasion. When there are vacancies in statewide offices, the governor must choose from three candidates selected by the central committee. This is how Karl Allred—a perennially unsuccessful candidate for state office and gas plant foreperson who illegally carried a gun onto the University of Wyoming's campus for the state party's convention one year—was selected as interim secretary of state.[36]

---

[35] See recent roll call votes, https://www.wyoming.gop/blog/categories/scc-meeting-role-call.

[36] Maggie Mullen, "Gov. Gordon Appoints Karl Allred Interim Secretary of State," WyoFile, September 30, 2022, https://wyofile.com/gov-gordon-appoints-karl-allred-interim-secretary-of-state/.

The new right's obsession with enhancing the power of rural Wyoming is related to its identification with the working class and alienation from the state's professional class. Even so, the share of college-educated citizens in the state's two most urbanized counties is only modestly higher than in the state's hinterlands (see Table 1.1). Unsurprisingly, the two most highly educated counties are solidly blue: uber-rich Teton and Albany, home to the state's only college town. Laramie County is relatively well educated but only somewhat. Some deep red rural counties, like Johnson, Park, and Sheridan, can boast similar levels of college education. Likewise, Natrona and Laramie are only somewhat wealthier than the average rural county.

The figures in Table 1.1 also show that many Wyoming communities enjoy good median incomes despite fairly low levels of college education. Wyoming has long been a place where high school graduates can earn a family wage in the state's energy sector. Social mobility also remains high in the Equality State. One recent study concluded: "Overall, Wyoming's economic structure has provided a high quality of life for many residents and an enviable level of equity and social mobility."[37]

This evidence, at first glance, suggests the establishment is right: The rural counties' war against Laramie and Natrona rests on an illusion. There is no sharp urban–rural divide in Wyoming, no geographic divide between common folk and city folk. When we asked Joe McGinley, currently the state committeeman for the Natrona County GOP, about these rural grievances, he did not mince words. "Their narrative" is "totally untrue," he said. He reminded us that Natrona includes a lot of rural Wyoming, not just the small city of Casper. "There are ranchers and farmers here in Natrona County just like there are in every other county," he added.

What McGinley neglects to notice, though, is that because of Natrona's and Laramie's size, they are home to a much larger community of college-educated professionals and that fact shapes *the face* of these

37 Thảo-Nguyên Bùi et al., "A Growth Perspective on Wyoming," CID Faculty Working Paper No. 432 (Harvard University, March 2023), 5. See also Richard V. Reeves and Eleanor Krause, "Raj Chetty in 14 Charts: Big Findings on Opportunity and Mobility We Should All Know," Brookings Institution, January 11, 2018, https://www.brookings.edu/articles/raj-chetty-in-14-charts-big-findings-on-opportunity-and-mobility-we-should-know/.

Table 1.1 Education and Wealth of Wyoming Counties, 2023

	College education (percent of adults over 25)	Median household income	Poverty rate (percent of population)
Albany	55.9	$55,887	23.0
Big Horn	20.5	$61,262	11.1
Campbell	21.9	$93,315	9.5
Carbon	21.1	$65,196	12.3
Converse	22.0	$79,235	11.0
Crook	23.3	$68,876	6.3
Fremont	24.3	$60,030	13.9
Goshen	24.0	$62,356	9.3
Hot Springs	28.2	$64,031	16.1
Johnson	31.8	$60.667	16.7
Laramie	**30.5**	**$76,282**	**9.0**
Lincoln	23.1	$83,033	7.1
Natrona	**26.6**	**$69,104**	**9.1**
Niobrara	20.0	$54,375	18.3
Park	32.8	$66,754	9.6
Platte	22.1	$64,753	12.0
Sheridan	32.1	$68,898	8.7
Sublette	25.6	$85,960	8.1
Sweetwater	20.0	$79,375	11.7
Teton	60.3	$108,279	6.9
Uinta	19.1	$78,164	6.5
Washakie	21.1	$61,875	6.7
Weston	17.6	$71,800	12.9

Source: Wyoming Department of Administration and Information, "Wyoming and County Profiles 2023," http://eadiv.state.wy.us/demog_data/County_Profile.html.

local parties. Thus, their leadership posts are dominated by members of the professional class, especially lawyers. The party organizations in rural counties, meanwhile, are home to a much larger contingent of more modestly educated Wyomingites.

These rural–urban differences are also increasingly visible as Wyoming's Republican factions compete for power. Consider the case of Jared Olsen. He is married to Dani Olsen, chair of the Laramie delegation at the 2022 state GOP convention. A lawyer from Cheyenne, Olsen has been active in the Laramie County party. He was first elected to the state legislature in 2017, and after quickly ingratiating himself with the establishment leadership, he ascended to House minority whip in 2021. The following year Olsen seemed poised to become the majority floor leader. But in an election that sent shock waves through the GOP establishment, Olsen was beaten by Chip Neiman, a candidate with a high school education from Hulet, a town of 318 residents.[38] Olsen and Neiman are not just from different sides of the tracks—they are also partisans in Wyoming's Republican civil war. Olsen is an establishment Republican, reviled and distrusted by the new guard. He was "awarded" RINO of the Month in September of 2022.[39] Neiman, meanwhile, is a leader of the House Freedom Caucus.

Rural–urban differences also emerged in Cheney's primary race. While Cheney lost practically everywhere, she ran better in Natrona and Laramie Counties than in the state's more rural counties (see Table 1.2). And in the cities within Natrona and Laramie, she was even more competitive with Hageman. In the city of Cheyenne, for example, Cheney gathered approximately 45 percent of the vote.[40]

What's more, there are new signs of economic and social stress in rural Wyoming. While social mobility is higher than in many other American states, it's also on the decline.[41] And while Laramie's and Natrona's populations grew about 10 and 6 percent after the last census, respectively, most of the state's small rural areas are shedding people.

---

[38] Kerry Drake, "What the Rise of Wyoming's Freedom Caucus Means for Liberty," WyoFile, November 29, 2022, https://wyofile.com/what-the-rise-of-wyomings-freedom-caucus-means-for-liberty/.

[39] "RINO of the Month, September 2022," https://wyorino.com/rino-of-the-month-september-2022/.

[40] Calculated from these sources: "Laramie County Official Precinct-by-Precinct Summary Wyoming Primary Election," August 16, 2022, https://sos.wyo.gov/Elections/Docs/2022/Results/Primary/2022_Laramie_County_Primary_PbP.pdf; Laramie County Wyoming, "Voter and Precinct Information," https://maps.clcgisc.com/portal/apps/webappviewer/index.html?id=6c122e09faec455eab3a05f9e896448a.

[41] Bùi et al., "Growth Perspective on Wyoming," 60.

Table 1.2 Cheney Support in Natrona and
Laramie Counties, 2022 House Primary

Laramie	39%
Natrona	30%
Rural counties*	20%

*Teton and Albany, two Democratic-leaning counties, were excluded from the analysis.
Source: "Wyoming at-Large Congressional District Primary Election Results," New York Times, August 18, 2022, https://www.nytimes.com/interactive/2022/08/16/us/elections/results-wyoming-us-house-district-1.html.

And some are really hemorrhaging. Sublette—a county with fewer than 9,000 Wyomingites—lost 15 percent of its population in just a decade. Small Washakie County declined by nearly 10 percent and has lost nearly 20 percent of its residents since 1980. Meanwhile, Joey Correnti's Carbon County shed nearly 9 percent of its population. The one major exception to rural decline is Teton County, mostly home to affluent Democrats who reside in and around Jackson Hole.[42] Those population shifts are driven by larger economic forces. As economic growth and opportunity expand in cities and shrink in small towns, people leave the latter for the former. And those who leave are often these towns' best and brightest young people.[43]

Perhaps most distressingly, the state's suicide rate has nearly doubled since 2005, leaving it with the highest rate in the nation.[44] It is also astonishingly high in some of Wyoming's most rural counties. Hot Springs County, for example, has a suicide rate that is more than five times the national average. Meanwhile, Wyoming's two most urbanized

---

[42] Morgan Hughes, "Wyoming Gains 2.3% Population Over Decade; 14 Counties Lose Residents," Casper Star-Tribune, August 12, 2021, https://trib.com/news/state-and-regional/wyoming-gains-2-3-population-over-decade-14-counties-lose-residents/article_61101c77-f5e5-54ba-9c3f-a444921c1a35.html.

[43] On this development more generally, see Patrick J. Carr and Maria Kefalas, Hollowing Out the Middle: The Rural Brain Drain and What It Means for America (Beacon Press, 2009).

[44] Center for Disease Control and Prevention, "Suicide Mortality by State," https://www.cdc.gov/nchs/pressroom/sosmap/suicide-mortality/suicide.htm.

counties—Natrona and Laramie—have suicide rates that are below the state's average.[45]

Even healthy rural communities face structural inequalities larger places do not. Practically everything—including basic goods like medical care and schools—are more difficult to get to. Rural folks also spend more on gas because they do a lot of driving, about 59 percent more than urbanites, according to one estimate. Meanwhile, rural Americans are often poorer than urbanities and notice these regional inequalities. As political scientist Katherine Cramer observed: "[W]hen wealthy urban tourists visit economically challenged rural areas, the contrast in the standard of living is often rather blatant to the local residents."[46]

Though rural identity is entangled with class, it seems much more weakly connected to race, at least in Wyoming. Natrona and Laramie Counties are distrusted and reviled by rural party activists even though they are not more racially diverse than the state as a whole. Both counties are overwhelmingly white, and Black Americans are scarce in both places. Blacks constitute some 2.5 percent of residents in Laramie and 1.3 percent of residents in Natrona (see Table 1.3).[47] The face of the party is, unsurprisingly, nearly all white in every part of the state. There is only one Black member of the Wyoming legislature, but she is from the new right.[48]

That's not to say there isn't racism in the Wyoming Republican Party. Of course there is.[49] It just doesn't seem to explain the political divisions among conservatives. That means that even if there wasn't a drop of racism in the state, we would still expect to see essentially the same civil war inside the Republican Party.

---

[45] See data table from Wyoming's Department of Health, https://health.wyo.gov/wp-content/uploads/2021/10/2020ARD09-Suicide-Rate.pdf.

[46] Cramer, *Politics of Resentment*, 101–4.

[47] US Census Bureau, "Quick Facts: Laramie County, Wyoming," https://www.census.gov/quickfacts/laramiecountywyoming.

[48] See Senator Profile of Lynn Hutchings, https://www.wyoleg.gov/Legislators/2023/S/1997.

[49] About 8 percent of the American adult population are white nationalists, according to Marc Hetherington and Jonathan Weiler, *Prius or Pickup? How the Answers to Four Simple Questions Explain America's Great Divide* (Houghton Mifflin Harcourt, 2018), 43–44.

Table 1.3 Racial Demographics of
Wyoming Counties, 2023

	White*	Black	Hispanic
Albany	82.2	1.5	10.0
Big Horn	86.0	0.9	10.2
Campbell	86.4	0.7	9.3
Carbon	76.5	1.2	18.7
Converse	87.9	0.7	8.7
Crook	93.0	0.9	3.5
Fremont	69.3†	0.7	8.2
Goshen	84.4	1.3	11.5
Hot Springs	89.6	1.2	4.7
Johnson	89.7	0.9	5.5
Laramie	77.5	2.5	15.8
Lincoln	91.3	0.6	5.4
Natrona	85.6	1.3	9.6
Niobrara	89.3	1.0	5.2
Park	90.1	0.7	6.3
Platte	87.7	0.7	8.5
Sheridan	91.0	0.7	5.2
Sublette	88.8	0.9	6.8
Sweetwater	78.8	1.3	16.6
Teton	79.9	0.8	15.8
Uinta	86.6	0.7	10.1
Washakie	82.1	0.5	14.2
Weston	88.6	0.8	5.5

* Excludes Hispanics who self-identify as white. † Fremont
County is home to a large Native American reservation.
Source: Wyoming Department of Administration and Information, "Wyoming and County Profiles 2023," http://eadiv.
state.wy.us/demog_data/County_Profile.html.

Even beyond Wyoming, there is good evidence that rural identity
politics would thrive without racism. In fact, we see the same divides
in countries without our racial divisions. Support for the Conservative Party in Canada, for example, is reliably predicted by geography.
Stanford political scientist Jonathan Rodden finds that the city of

Winnipeg is typical. Its "urban core . . . still votes reliably for the parties of the left, but the Conservative vote share increases rapidly as one leaves the city center." According to Rodden, the relationship between population density and voting is so powerful, it functions like a natural law. Much "like a fractal in the natural sciences or mathematics," Rodden explains, it "repeats itself at every scale."[50]

Turning to the United States, the drive to retain rural voting power wasn't connected to the campaign to maintain white supremacy, even prior to the landmark civil rights victories of the 1960s. As Stephen Ansolabehere and James Snyder found, this is partly because "southern blacks were distributed fairly evenly between urban and rural counties." That was true outside the south as well. "Malapportionment," they note, did not "contribute to the systematic disenfranchisement of blacks and Hispanics." The old overrepresentation of rural communities, however, did empower poorer Americans. As the same study found, "Counties with higher income were more likely to be undercounted than counties with lower income, and the correlations are very strong."[51]

Nor is Trump's rise evidently driven by a mobilization of racial resentment, despite his incendiary racial rhetoric. Recent scholarship has found that while Trump did attract a relatively small group of whites with high racial resentment scores, those voters have long voted for Republicans and are a shrinking slice of the electorate. Instead, Trump won in 2016 because he attracted a much larger share of white voters who were racial moderates.[52] Most of these supporters were attracted to Trump for other reasons.[53]

---

[50] Jonathan Rodden, *Why Cities Lose: The Deep Roots of the Urban–Rural Divide* (Basic Books, 2019), 52, 121.

[51] Ansolabehere and Snyder, *End of Inequality*, 85–86.

[52] Justin Grimer et al., "Measuring the Contribution of Voting Blocs to Election Outcomes," SocArXiv, June 26, 2022, https://osf.io/preprints/socarxiv/c9fkg.

[53] For other explanations see, for example, Ben Enke, "Moral Values and Voting: Trump and Beyond," NBER Working Paper 24268 (National Bureau of Economic Research, January 2018), https://www.nber.org/system/files/working_papers/w24268/revisions/w24268.revo.pdf; Benjamin Enke, "Moral Values and Voting," *Journal of Political Economy* 128, no. 10 (2020): 3679–729; Muravchik and Shields, *Trump's*

Trump also didn't mobilize rural identity in Wyoming (although he benefited from it in his battle with Cheney). Nor can its origins be traced to the Tea Party. As the decades-long fight over redistricting makes plain, rural counties in Wyoming have long resented the larger, wealthier counties. When we asked John Brown, a party activist from rural Fremont County, about rural grievances, he said, "Yeah, the small counties have always had a bug up their ass about the large counties."

* * * * *

Even if rural consciousness is old in Wyoming, the new right consciously placed rural grievances and identity at the center of its movement. Doing so didn't just provide some meaningful form to the new, expressive identity politics. It was also useful. After all, the leaders of the new right understand that establishment Republicans are well ensconced in the state's two largest counties, Natrona and Laramie. Thus, it hardly matters that these counties are not, in fact, home to large metropolises that are controlled by socially liberal RINOs. They are still home to their enemies. And in politics, perception matters more than reality.

Rural resentments are also easier to mobilize in an era where the major parties are increasingly divided along the lines of social geography. As liberalization has become increasingly identified in the public mind with urbanites, it may be easier for some Wyomingites to regard Republicans residing in Casper and Cheyenne with suspicion, particularly when they resist reforms that would redistribute political power out into the countryside. Plus, it's hardly unusual for identity politics in homogeneous communities to make a lot out of minor differences. Because it is obsessed with authenticity—a quality that is easily contaminated—slight differences readily become "problematic."

Authenticity in Wyoming isn't just about ruralness, though. In the next chapter we turn to another source of the identity essential to the new right: social class.

Democrats; Thomas Ferguson et al., "The Economic and Social Roots of Populist Rebellion: Support for Donald Trump in 2016," Working Paper No. 83 (Institute for New Economic Thinking, October 2018).

2

The Class War

IN 1956 JEAN SHEPARD, A New York jazz musician and late-night disc jockey on station WOR, took to the airwaves to praise the novel *I, Libertine* by Frederick Ewing. To entice his listeners Shepard told them that Ewing is "well remembered" for his talks on "erotica of the 18th century." It seemed to work. Many of Shepard's listeners—both in the United States and abroad—marched to their local bookstores to purchase Ewing's novel. They all struck out, though, and for good reason: Ewing and his novel were made up. The hoax caught the attention of the science fiction novelist Theodore Sturgeon. He had an idea. Since the fictitious work had become the talk of elite society, Sturgeon decided to write a novel titled *I, Libertine* to capitalize on its buzz.[1] It worked. The real *I, Libertine* became a bestseller.

Mostly long forgotten, the affair caught the attention of another provocative radio personality 66 years later, just as Liz Cheney's primary race was beginning to heat up. Glenn Woods, the right-wing host of the popular *Wake Up Wyoming*, regaled his listeners with Shepard's hoax, though not as an example of the mass media's ability to spread disinformation. To Woods it was a parable about the arrogance

---

[1] Cater Henderson, "Night People's Hoax on Day People Makes Hit with Book Folks," *Wall Street Journal*, August 1, 1956.

and phoniness of college-educated professionals. After all, Shepard had duped many highly educated elites into praising and celebrating a book that didn't exist. Elites in our day, Woods thought, often pretend to be knowing, just like those ridiculous urbane professionals searching for Ewing's novel in Manhattan bookstores way back in the 1950s.

Thus, Woods told his listeners that Shepard revealed something important: "He exposed these lying, elitist, ignorant, stupid—I can't pick enough words to describe [them]—[that] really showed them for who they really are, from the news media to the politicians to the bureaucrats to college professors." Needless to say these fakers, Woods went on to add, should not be considered "the smart ones among us, the leaders among us." They should just take those degrees and shove it. As Woods put it: "Screw your degree!"[2]

That Wyoming's most popular right-wing radio personality would devote a show to dumping on the professional class says something important about Republican politics today. Like the major parties themselves, the GOP is also coming apart by social class—and Cheney's defeat at the hands of Trump's proxy candidate Harriet Hageman was a symptom of this bigger reality, a tip of a larger iceberg.

Her loss represents a further repudiation of Wyoming's old guard Republicans—a once comfortable establishment steeped in the cultural world of professional, college-educated elites. It also represents a victory for Wyoming's new, Trump-styled insurgents, who, like Glenn Woods, tend to see Wyoming's Republican establishment as a class apart, as an alienating and corrupt aristocracy. To many of the new types, Woods got it right: These elites don't deserve to rule.

A Wyoming poll of likely Republican voters just days before Cheney's primary highlighted the growing class divide. In a step fashion, every incremental increase in education pushed Republican support for Cheney upward (see Table 2.1). While a mere 13 percent of Wyomingites with high school degrees or less said they intended to vote for Cheney, a majority of the most educated Republicans planned to do so. Her base was centered in Wyomingites with postgraduate degrees, which preferred Cheney by a margin of almost 2–1. As we'll see, that world is increasingly estranged from the party it once controlled.

---

[2] *Wake Up Wyoming with Glenn Woods* show, March 16, 2022.

Table 2.1 Candidate Preference in Wyoming Republican Primary, August 2022

	High school or less	Some college	BA	Graduate degree
Cheney	13%	20%	30%	56%
Hageman	73%	67%	55%	35%
Don't know	13%	10%	10%	8%

Source: Data from the Wyoming Primary Election Survey, 2022. Crosstabs run by Professor Jim King.

With Trump leading the way, this class cleavage is remaking the party outside of Wyoming as well. Trump cruised to the 2024 nomination thanks to the support of Republicans without college degrees. In the early presidential primaries and caucuses—including in Iowa, New Hampshire, and South Carolina—a majority of college-educated voters supported candidates other than Trump.[3] Only later, once Trump became the presumptive nominee, did the diploma divide narrow. Nationally, though, college-educated Republicans preferred a nominee other than Trump. A 2022 *New York Times* poll, for example, found that 63 percent of college-educated Republicans were ready to move on from the ex-president. But that same poll found that roughly the same percentage of Republicans remained loyal to their exiled king.[4]

To understand why Trump—and other Republican politicians from privilege—can emerge as heroes of the working class, it's critical not to think about class in narrowly economic terms. Class is as much about culture as it is about economics. It shapes our manners, aesthetics, and morals.[5] Thus, working-class culture is sometimes adopted by those with high-paying jobs and college degrees. At times, it is just

---

3 CNN, "Exit Poll Results for 2024 Presidential Primaries and Caucuses," https://www.cnn.com/election/2024/primaries-and-caucuses/exit-polls/north-carolina/republican-primary/president/0.

4 Poll by the *New York Times*/Siena College Research Institute, July 5–7, 2022, https://int.nyt.com/data/documenttools/us0722-crosstabs-all/6c241a3f5e5578a2/full.pdf.

5 On the cultural basis of class, see Pierre Bourdieu, *Distinction: A Social Critique of the Judgement of Taste* (Harvard University Press, 1984).

an opportunistic act, like US Senator John Fetterman pretending he's never heard the term "crudité." But in other cases, elite attachment to working-class culture is not just for show.

It certainly isn't for Trump. He could be the poster child for what our fellow members of the professional class would call "déclassé." So many of his tastes and behaviors—from his garish homes to his volatile marriages to his brash straight talk—signal his social proximity to Americans with middling educations and fortunes. More than that, these low- to middlebrow qualities signal Trump's distance from the highly educated professional class, a world that is increasingly detached from the mores of America's broad middle.

This is also why higher education—rather than income—is a better marker of social class, and the class cleavage within the GOP. A Republican electrician, after all, certainly earns far more than a Democratic graduate student in sociology, but the aspiring academic often looks down upon the social milieu of the skilled tradesperson. Similarly, the tradesperson is more likely to consider the culture of elite graduate schools to be effete, emasculated, and haughty. Such voters have been fleeing the Democratic Party as well as left-wing parties across the West. As one study of citizens in 21 democracies found, voters with relatively high incomes but low levels of education have been abandoning parties on the political left.[6]

These class differences shape Wyoming's Republican civil war. Their clashing visions of politics are inflected by different, class-based cultural understandings. For the governing conservatives in the old guard, politics requires values dear to their social class, including civility and deference to the expertise of credentialed professionals and seasoned lawmakers. The new insurgents, though, look upon these values as markers of elites' social distance from middle America and, ultimately, as tools of exclusion. For them, cursing and packing heat in the legislature may intimidate the old guard, but doing so is also a genuine expression of their class-based identities.

---

[6] Herbert P. Kitschelt and Philipp Rehm, "Polarity Reversal: The Socioeconomic Reconfiguration of Partisan Support in Knowledge Societies," *Politics & Society* 51, no. 4 (2023): 520–66.

As we'll see, these identities rest on a masculinized honor culture that prizes aggression and toughness, especially in men. The new types regard their expressions of crudeness and rugged strength as evidence that they are authentic conservatives, the state's rightful rulers. Now that these practitioners of class-based identity politics are working their way into positions of power in Wyoming, they are remaking old political norms in the party and legislature.

Of course, this Republican class war also mirrors and is nested within a much larger diploma divide that is polarizing our major parties.[7] Democrats are increasingly becoming the party of the professional class and are associated with its softer, more feminized norms and policies. That means that Wyoming's old guard faces a difficult political challenge, particularly in an age of political polarization: They must defend a way of doing politics that is increasingly linked to the detested Democratic Party.

* * * * *

Once dominated by a small group of affluent ranchers and college-educated members of the professional class, Wyoming's party elite had long cultivated and protected a culture marked by civility and gentlemanly grace. Ron Micheli embodied the old traditions. He served in the Wyoming House from 1977 until 1992 and then as the state's director of agriculture. When Republican candidates ran for statewide office, they would always stop at the Michelis' home where they would dine and stay the night. Ron would even welcome those he didn't endorse. That made a big impression on his son Matt, who would later become the chair of the state GOP. "That's the Wyoming I grew up in. That's the Wyoming I love," Matt told us.

Others remember the once unquestioned culture with a wistful fondness too. Tom Walters, a state representative from Casper, recalled the 1990 race for governor, which pitted Republican Mary Mead against Democrat Mike Sullivan. In his telling, Mary showed up to the

---

7 Doug Sosnik, "The 'Diploma Divide' Is the New Fault Line in American Politics," *New York Times*, April 17, 2023; Joshua N. Zingher, "Diploma Divide: Educational Attainment and the Realignment of the American Electorate," *Political Research Quarterly* 75, no. 2 (2022): 10659129221079862; Matt Grossman and David A. Hopkins, *Divided by Degrees: How the Diploma Divide and the Culture War Transformed American Politics* (Cambridge University Press, 2024).

inaugural ball to dance with Mike even though she lost the race. "To me," Walters said, "that's the epitome of Wyoming politics."

Thus, the old party mandarins were the custodians of this culture and took pride in it. Nick Reynolds, a local journalist, told us that the political culture in Wyoming has traditionally been "dictated from the top down." "The leadership [in the state legislature] has this reverence for the institution. They are just so steeped in its traditions and in the decorum of the legislature." It was a world until itself.

But it was always fragile. Most Wyomingites lived in a different culture, one that is generally familiar to citizens outside the professional class. Social scientists call it "honor culture," though ordinary citizens have given it many names: the "code of the street" in poor urban neighborhoods, "hillbilly justice" in Appalachia, and the "code of the West" in Western states like Wyoming.[8] They are particularly prevalent in white towns outside of the nation's metropolitan centers.[9] Americans who reside in places where such cultures prevail must always respond to aggression—and signal to everyone that they shouldn't be messed with. There is no ignoring any slight in an honor culture. Doing so risks being read as weak, and that makes one vulnerable to challengers.

Honor cultures are common throughout the world because they grow in places marked by insecurity. In the absence of modern institutions that regulate violence and conflict—including courts, police, and the rule of law—people have relied on their reputations for toughness to ward off aggressors.

Those premodern conditions characterized much of the American West, including Wyoming. In Wyoming's Johnson County a 4-year range war erupted in 1889 between cattle companies and local settlers. The fighting, which was driven by conflicts over land and water, culminated in scores of deaths. It didn't subside until the US Cavalry

---

[8] See, for example, Elijah Anderson, *Code of the Street: Decency, Violence, and the Moral Life of the Inner City* (W. W. Norton and Company, 2000); J. D. Vance, *Hillbilly Elegy* (Harper, 2016); Richard E. Nisbet and Dov Cohen, *Culture of Honor: The Psychology of Violence in the American South* (Taylor and Francis, 1996); Stephanie Muravchik and Jon A. Shields, *Trump's Democrats* (Brookings, 2020).

[9] Ryan Brown, *Honor Bound: How a Cultural Ideal Has Shaped the American Psyche* (Oxford University Press, 2016), 66.

intervened on the orders of President Benjamin Harrison.[10] Cultures, though, often persist long after the conditions that created them disappear—and that is true of Wyoming's honor culture.

Wyoming's political class has always had to navigate this rougher, working-class world outside its professional circles. A young Dick Cheney had to do so in his Casper high school. When Dick's teacher caught him fighting, Cheney wasn't suspended. Instead, his teacher required Dick and his combatant to resolve their grudge in a boxing match, held at the end of the year. Dick sought out a boxing coach to help him prepare for the duel. The school sold tickets for the showdown, and the proceeds from the event went to the school booster club. Apparently, the boxing lessons were a good investment. Dick won the match.[11]

No Wyoming politician was better at navigating this honor culture than the famed Al Simpson, who served first in the Wyoming statehouse before ascending to the US Senate. Like any gifted politician, Senator Simpson could code-switch. He adopted a more genteel code for his life in Washington and another, when needed, on the campaign trail in Wyoming. Simpson understood that one can never back down from a fight without losing the respect of one's constituents. So, when one local began complaining about his veteran's benefits, Senator Simpson didn't say, "I'm sorry. I'll look into it." Instead, Simpson threw some rhetoric counterpunches, as recounted in Stephen Hayes' biography of Dick Cheney:

> "How long did you serve?" Simpson asked his inquisitor.
> "None of your business," the man responded. It was not the right answer.
> "Yes it is," Simpson thundered. "I bet you never left Camp Beetle Bailey."
> "I served eight months," stammered the man. Not good enough, said Simpson.

---

[10] John W. Davis, *Wyoming Range War: The Infamous Invasion of Johnson County* (University of Oklahoma Press, 2010).

[11] Stephen F. Hayes, *Cheney: The Untold Story of America's Most Powerful and Controversial Vice President* (HarperCollins, 2007), 24–25.

"I served overseas for two years and you don't know either end of a mortar from your asshole. In my opinion you've already taken too much of the government's money."

Simpson didn't stop there. He concluded by suggesting that this constituent was seeking medical care not because of his military service but because he fell off a barstool.[12]

Though this sort of code-switching often goes unnoticed by the media and scholars, the best politicians in both parties practice it, especially when they're campaigning in working-class communities where honor cultures prevail. President Joe Biden is a good example. When Biden campaigned in New Hampton, Iowa, a citizen accused him of corruption and being too old to seek the presidency. Like Simpson, Biden didn't back down. He called the man "a damned liar" and then challenged him to a push-up contest.[13] Critics saw it as just another Biden gaffe, but they don't understand American honor culture like Biden does. The Iowans gave him a big round of applause.[14]

When politicians enter elite circles, such as their legislatures or fancy fundraisers, they enter another world. It's one governed by different norms, generally more civil and deliberative. In the US Congress, for example, representatives are customarily called the "gentleman" from California or the "gentlewoman" for New York when floor business is being conducted.

In the Wyoming legislature and the state party, the old culture is being challenged by new elected officials and party activists who reject the old norms. One is state senator Anthony Bouchard, first elected in 2016. Although guns are not allowed in the statehouse, Bouchard insisted on keeping one strapped to his hip. As he once told his supporters: "Politicians will not respect you unless they fear you."[15] Bouchard

[12] Hayes, *Cheney*, 187–88.

[13] "Watch Joe Biden Call Iowa Man a 'Damn Liar,'" YouTube, 1 min., 43 sec., https://www.youtube.com/watch?v=MrL4Pcz-DiQ.

[14] Stephanie Muravchik and Jon A. Shields, "Those Biden 'Gaffes'? Some Voters Actually Like Them," *New York Times*, September 16, 2020, https://www.nytimes.com/2020/09/16/opinion/biden-obama-trump-voters.html.

[15] Nick Reynolds, "Anti-Vaxxers Commandeer Committee Meeting to Protest Mandates," WyoFile, September 20, 2021, https://wyofile.com/anti-vaxxers-commandeer-committee-meeting-to-protest-mandates/.

does his best to make sure they do. He even insisted that Anthony Fauci should be executed. The only question was how. "After prosecution, the chair, the gallows, or lethal injection?" Bouchard wondered.[16]

Senator Bouchard is hardly alone. Guns, once a rarity at the GOP state convention and other party meetings, are now commonplace. At the 2022 state convention, one delegate was even more primed for battle: He strutted about with a fully cocked gun on his hip.

Sometimes violence even breaks out at the convention. In 2020, there was a fistfight between two county chairs, sending one to the hospital with a dislocated shoulder and broken ankle. Joey Correnti, who won the scrape, likes to remind others he's not to be messed with. He packs a gun on both hips and carries an ax handle.[17] With a note of pride, Correnti told us: "I am a sledgehammer."

He is hardly the only sledgehammer these days. After the COVID outbreak, a county commissioner meeting to discuss masking was shut down because health officials were being yelled at. Troy Bray, a precinct committeeman from Park County, even called a female state senator a "cunt" because she voted against an anti-vaccine mandate bill. Bray added, for good measure: "If I were as despicable a person as you, I would kill myself to rid the world of myself. You sicken me."[18] Under fire for his remarks, Bray did apologize, before walking it back. Now he reportedly sports a T-shirt that says: "I was right, she is a cunt," all because she didn't support an anti-vaccine bill.

The threat of violence hangs over candidate events as well. In 2022, the far-right group "Liberty's Place 4 U Wyoming" hosted a candidate forum, which attracted politicians seeking local and statewide office. Before the event, the emcee felt compelled to offer this admonition:

[16] Nick Reynolds, "Bouchard Calls for Fauci to Be Tried Then Executed," WyoFile, September 10, 2021, https://wyofile.com/bouchard-calls-for-fauci-to-be-tried-then-executed/.

[17] Nick Reynolds, "Gillette Police Cite Albany County GOP Chair, Say He Instigated Fight That Left Him in Hospital," Casper Star-Tribune, June 29, 2020, https://trib.com/news/state-and-regional/govt-and-politics/gillette-police-cite-albany-county-gop-chair-say-he-instigated-fight-that-left-him-in/article_d5103933-6594-5987-a748-e7b1aa2c78ff.html.

[18] Associated Press, "Incivility, Disrespect on Rise in Wyoming Politics," U.S. News & World Report, December 11, 2021, https://www.usnews.com/news/best-states/wyoming/articles/2021-12-11/incivility-disrespect-on-rise-in-wyoming-politics.

"Remember, no physical altercations. . . . Remember, the sheriff is still here." No violence broke out that evening, though there was plenty of heckling and yelling.[19]

In the Natrona County party, still a bastion of the old guard, many of the regulars feel intimidated by the new political climate. Once Correnti showed up at one of its party meetings as a self-appointed diplomat to settle a dispute between the state party and Natrona. Nick Reynolds, a local journalist, recalled that Correnti had his hatchet and a massive handgun on his hip. "It was clear that people were intimidated. You could see it on the executive committee's faces."

Others we spoke with confirmed Nick's report. Susan Stubson, an activist in the Natrona County party, said she finds all the guns and bravado threatening. So does JoAnn True, who is also involved in the Natrona County GOP. She was exhausted by the chilly climate inside the 2022 state convention. "You feel it in rooms like that," she told us. It marked a sharp contrast to her first state convention, back in 2010, when the old culture still prevailed. "It had a family reunion feel to it," JoAnn recalled. "People would be excited to get together. It was a much more festive atmosphere."

True and many others in the old guard blame the loss of that atmosphere on outsiders who moved to the state in recent years, bringing a toxic national political culture with them. As one representative from the old guard told us: "Every year a few more people are elected who are not from Wyoming and bring their style of politics with them. They didn't like where they came from."

There is truth to the assertion. One new Freedom Caucus member, Representative Jeannette Ward, for example, recently moved away from Illinois seeking relief from COVID mask mandates. She calls herself "a political refugee."[20] Some of the prominent architects of the new politics, including Anthony Bouchard and Joey Correnti, are from out

---

[19] Victoria Eavis, "At Raucous Forum, Candidates Make Their Case to Voters," *Casper Star-Tribune*, June 3, 2022, https://trib.com/news/local/casper/at-raucous-forum-candidates-make-their-case-to-voters/article_b7d2d942-e378-11ec-8a1a-ffd2b2921d42.html.

[20] Jasmine Hall, "Who Is Honor Wyoming?" *Jackson Hole News and Guide*, May 8, 2024.

of state. And their numbers have swelled in recent years, as Chapter 4 will show.[21]

Others blame Trump. One old-line Republican, who insisted on remaining anonymous, told us: "That is absolutely part of the Trump effect.... They think they can win by being like Trump." "It has trickled all the way down to your local school board." "So, you get people who think the more obnoxious you can be," he added, "that's what it takes to win." Landon Brown, a state representative from Cheyenne, agrees. Brown noted that local candidates "see that it's acceptable" to behave like Trump, the beloved leader of the party. In this way, such observers believe Trump has defined deviance down.

Both explanations suggest that a nationalization of Wyoming politics is at work, where candidates from outside the state are changing local norms. That is certainly the case. But it's also true that Wyoming's political culture was always a subculture even within the state, removed in many ways from more working-class sensibilities, especially a local honor culture.

The Stubsons, one of Wyoming's power couples, see this truth more clearly than many of their friends and allies. Tim and Susan are lawyers from Casper. Susan serves in the Natrona County party; Tim ran for the US House unsuccessfully in 2016. Even though Tim was defeated by Liz Cheney in that race, both were outspoken supporters of her—and are appalled by the current drift of the party. That drift, though, has made it easier for them to see the social and cultural insularity of the old party.

When we asked them whether it was common to pack heat at state conventions in the past, Tim said it wasn't, largely because the party was dominated by a different class of people: "No, you were talking businessmen and ranchers and bankers. It's [become] a much more blue-collar party. Many of those old stalwarts have been pushed out." "Those folks were critical to the conversation and tenor of the party," Susan added. "This is not what I've been building. It's not for me." Thus, the Stubsons don't simply blame out-of-state interlopers for corrupting their

[21] See, for example, Leo Wolfson, "Move to Wyoming and Then Instantly Run for Legislature Is a Real Trend," *Cowboy State Daily*, June 6, 2024.

indigenous political culture. As Tim conceded: "there was a current there that we were not aware of."

For all their differences, Joey Correnti sees the conflict in class terms as well. When we sat down with Joey at the state GOP convention, he delighted in telling us his crowd "broke the old establishment, the old bluebloods." For Correnti, class isn't just, or even primarily, about interests. It's about a set of norms that should govern the conflict of interests. With a laugh, Correnti told us that there is "way too much dignity around here [the party]!" The old establishment, he said, calls his crowd "uncouth," but, in fact, the "elitists" who make these accusations are simply puffed up with "false pride." For Correnti, then, the establishment's enchantment with civility doesn't have a higher purpose; instead, it's primarily a tool of exclusion and class snobbery.

A favorite target of Correnti is Joe McGinley, a leader of the Natrona County party and defender of the old politics. As a Stanford-educated physician with a thriving practice, McGinley makes for an ideal symbol of the establishment's distance from commoners like Correnti. Correnti claims that his nemesis introduces himself as "*Doctor* Joe McGinley"—an outward sign of his class-based haughtiness. Like the much reviled Dr. Fauci, Correnti sees McGinley as little more than an empty suit, a man unworthy of his respect and deference.

Resentment toward those in the professional class is common in middle America. As the left-wing writer Barbara Ehrenreich recalled the typical working-class prejudices of her family: "My father . . . could not say the word doctor without the virtual prefix *quack*. Lawyers were *shysters*, as in *shyster-lawyer*; and professors were without exception *phonies*."[22] Sociologist Michele Lamont's classic study of working-class men shows that Ehrenreich's father is not idiosyncratic. The men Lamont interviewed described members of the professional class as "snobby" and "fake." One police officer she interviewed said he didn't like "people with facades or snotty people. I just like regular people. I don't try to hang out with lawyers and doctors."[23]

---

[22] Barabra Ehrenreich, *Fear of Falling: The Inner Life of the Middle Class* (Twelve, 2020), 162.

[23] Michelle Lamont, *The Dignity of Working Men: Morality and the Boundaries of Race, Class and Immigration* (Russell Sage Foundation, 2000), 107–12.

Legal sociologist Joan Williams suspects that everyday life reinforces these prejudices. As she notes, middle Americans often "suffer class afronts from professionals every day: the doctor who unthinkingly patronizes the medical technician, the harried office worker who treats the security guard as invisible, the overbooked business traveler who snaps at the TSA agent."[24]

Some in the old guard believe that Correnti's class war is mostly contrived by some newcomers grasping for power. They observe that the architects of the new politics are themselves highly educated. That is certainly true of some of them. Representative Chuck Gray is a good example. Though he casts himself as a political outsider fighting for Wyoming's commoners, Gray received an MBA from the University of Pennsylvania. So is Harriet Hageman—the challenger who unseated Liz Cheney in 2022. She is a lawyer and former member of Cheney's clique, not to mention the daughter of a prominent rancher and politician from the old school. Ever attuned to new conservative insurgents, Hageman's first campaign ad appealed to the state's deeply rooted honor culture. It accused Liz Cheney of breaking the "code of the West," one that requires both "honor" and a willingness to "fight" for fellow partisans.[25]

Some Republican elites, though, still have a feel and affection for the rougher, lower-middle-class neighborhoods they grew up in. Nationally, such conservative figures include Rudy Giuliani, Chris Christie, and J. D. Vance. For them, appealing to the cultural sensibilities of working-class Americans may come easier than it does for opportunists like Hageman. And unlike Al Simpson—a Republican from the old guard who had a gift for code-switching when campaigning necessitated it—the new Republicans sought to change the norms of politics more generally.

None more so, of course, than Donald Trump. Raised in Queens, Trump imbibed the honor culture of his youth. Afterward, his dealings in the rough-and-tumble world of New York real estate and casino-building in Atlantic City probably confirmed the importance of being

---

[24] Joan C. Williams, *White Working Class: Overcoming Class Cluelessness in America* (Harvard Business Review Press, 2017), 26.

[25] Hageman for Wyoming, "Ride for the Brand," YouTube, 2 min., 15 sec., https://www.youtube.com/watch?v=egPY884jF64&t=26s.

feared. As Bob Woodward once described Trump's one guiding principle: "Never show weakness. You've always got to be strong. Don't be
bullied. There is no choice."[26]

More generally, Trump's tastes are distinctly middlebrow. His pent-
house in Trump Tower—an almost comically garish dwelling, full
of gold, marble, and mirrors—is what David Brooks' "bobos" would
consider déclassé. The same is true of his hotels, not to mention Mar-a-
Lago. When Trump purchased this "winter White House," he remod-
eled it to reflect his tastes, transforming it into an estate that one typical
member of the professional class described as "disgustingly gaudy."[27]

New right politicians, though, are not just a privileged lot, pander-
ing to the lower-middle class. In Wyoming, the new conservatism has
done something truly admirable in this new gilded age of American politics: It has brought more genuinely working-class politicians into the
legislature. Examples include Bill Fortner (a welder by trade), Bill Allemand (owner of a small trucking company), Pepper Ottman (4th-grade
teacher's aid), Ken Pendergraft (contractor), Clarence Styvar (supervi-
sor for the railroad), and Chip Neiman (small business owner), none of
whom are college graduates.

According to our analysis, roughly half of the new right members in Wyoming's legislature do not have a 4-year college degree (see
Table 2.2). Their numbers are also growing fast. In 2022 alone, five
new conservatives without college diplomas were elected to Wyoming's
House.[28] Some of these new right legislators did receive some voca-
tional education, but they are certainly not members of the college-
educated, professional class. For example, Mark Jennings, elected in
2015, has a degree in machine maintenance. And Daniel Singh, elected
in 2023, received an associate's degree at Calvary Chapel Bible College.

Meanwhile, very few members of Wyoming's Republican establishment came from comparable backgrounds. Of the 47 members we

---

[26] Bob Woodward, *Fear: Trump in the White House* (Simon and Schuster, 2018),
175–76.

[27] Mary Finn, "I Took My Trump-Loving Father to Mar-a-Lago," *Baltimore
Sun*, June 16, 2017, https://www.baltimoresun.com/citypaper/bcpnews-i-took-my-
trump-loving-father-to-mar-a-lago-20170616-story.html.

[28] They include Bill Allemand, Abby Angelos, Ken Pendergraft, Daniel Singh, and
Clarence Styvar.

Table 2.2 Republicans in Wyoming Statehouse with 4-Year College Degrees, June 2024

	House		Senate		Overall	
	New guard	Old guard	New guard	Old guard	New guard	Old guard
With degree	10	31	4	13	14	42
Without degree	10	2	6	3	16	5

Source: We used data from the website Honor Wyoming to identify new and old right conservatives. It's a partisan site affiliated with the new right that uses legislators' voting records to distinguish the "truly" conservative legislators from the RINOs (Republicans in name only). Those Honor Wyoming labeled as "high integrity" were classified as "new guard" Republicans for the purposes of this analysis. Similarly, those labeled "low integrity" were classified as "old guard" Republicans. Nine Republican legislators labeled "questionable integrity" were more ambiguous cases, and thus were not included in our analysis.

identified, only five did not have college degrees. And unlike the new right, many also earned postgraduate degrees: Nine have law degrees, several have master's degrees (two from Harvard), another has a PhD in economics, and one has a doctorate in veterinary medicine. In contrast, postgraduate degrees are rare among the new right legislators—and *not a single one* possesses a law degree.

The professional backgrounds of old guard Republicans make them much more similar to their Democratic colleagues in the legislature than the new insurgents. Of Wyoming's seven Democratic legislators, three have doctorates, one has a master's, one has an MFA, and two have bachelor's. As we'll see, they have also become allies, fighting to protect the legislature's traditions and norms against new right Republicans.

While many of the new right legislators come from solidly lower-middle-class backgrounds, some managed to ascend from much more humble beginnings. One is Tom James, who spent some of his teenage years in foster care and successfully campaigned for a state Senate seat while he was delivering pizzas. James described himself bluntly: "I've been a grunt all my life, I've worked in the Trona mines. I've worked on the railroad." He saw his ascension to the Senate as a challenge to the professional-business backgrounds of most state politicians: "A lot of people that are running for office are normally running their own business. You have a lot of doctors, You have a lot of lawyers . . . a lot of government workers." James thinks his humble background appealed to voters who "normally come in with an expectation that I'm going to be some stereotypical politician, all pompous, and high and mighty, and all that kind of thing. So when I don't come across that way, they're thankful for that."

For all their success, such candidates have been less successful winning statewide office. While Karl Allred, a foreperson at a gas plant, did recently serve as interim secretary of state, that seat is now in the hands of Chuck Gray, a new right conservative with a degree from Penn. And Hageman, who currently holds Cheney's former House seat, has a law degree. Thus far, then, some of the best-educated conservatives from the new right have had more success landing in the state's highest offices.

The new politicians have clashed at times with the old norms that still prevail in the Wyoming legislature. "When I talk to people," Bill Fortner conceded, "I might not use the best choice of words." "My slang might just offend somebody."[29] Another acknowledged that the old guard doesn't approve of her "potty mouth." Others say more with their actions than their words. Karl Allred gained notoriety for taking his gun into Senate committee hearings. Before launching into a statement against some proposed tax increases, Allred, one journalist noted, "adjusted his belt and the holstered pistol" and then took his seat in front of the assembled lawmakers.[30]

State senator Tom James does not see such rough edges as mere style; he sees it as the hallmark of a purer and more representative politics. When asked about the Republican establishment, he said with feeling, "that's a lot of old money in there." "You can see by their voting record, [they're] not for the people's interest. It's for their interest or someone they know." Although many members of the old guard cherish their families' deep roots in the state, James—a newcomer—was the only person who not only discounted such pedigree but actively derided it, claiming: "some of the worst people that are most corrupt in the legislature are fourth-, fifth-, sixth-generation Wyomingites."

Party activists are also increasingly likely to come from such backgrounds. The chair of the state party, Frank Eathorne, previously worked as a Terminix pest exterminator.[31] He replaced Ryan Mulholland, who resigned his chair to take a job out of state at Google. And unlike Mulholland, Eathorne has no interest in enforcing the old gentility at party meetings. As Joe McGinley observed, Eathorne and his team simply refuse to control hostile behavior on the convention floor. "In fact, they encourage it. They'll allow two individuals to just yell at each other." When members of the state's biggest and most cosmopolitan GOP county delegation marched out of the 2022 convention in protest after being stripped of their voting rights, many delegates cheered. Eathorne observed the spectacle silently from the dais.

---

[29] Mike Koshmril, "Wyoming Senate Takes a Stand on Civility," WyoFile, March 14, 2022, https://wyofile.com/wyoming-senate-takes-a-stand-on-civility/.

[30] Andrew Graham, "GOP Official Goes Armed to Oppose Tax Cut," WyoFile, May 3, 2019, https://wyofile.com/gop-official-goes-armed-to-oppose-tax-increases/.

[31] Rone Tempest and Victoria Eavis, "Wyoming GOP Chairman Quietly Assumed Power as Party Fractured," WyoFile, May 20, 2022, https://wyofile.com/wyo-gop-chairman-quietly-assumed-power-as-party-fractured/

These changes predate Trump's rise, though they've certainly accelerated since 2016. Tea Party activists attracted national attention as early as 2009 for their unruly behavior in public forums. One victim of this new incivility was the former Democratic member of Congress Tim Bishop (NY), who had held hundreds of meetings in his district without any problems. But as Jeffrey Berry and Sarah Sobieraj report in *The Outrage Industry*, that all changed for Bishop at a meeting in June 2009. At that meeting, the "shouting and hostility of the crowd was such that police were called in to safely escort him to his car." Similarly, then Democratic representative Gene Taylor (MS) "was escorted out of a meeting by 'a protective phalanx of eight uniformed Jackson County Sherrifs.'"[32]

In these examples, though, elected officials are the victims of the new incivility. Now they are the perpetrators. The movement, once led by just angry activists, has made inroads into elected office and party institutions. And it has brought a new, more confrontational style of politics with it.

The rise of working-class GOP politicians is also hardly unique to Wyoming. The Colorado representative Lauren Boebert dropped out of high school when she got pregnant. Later she earned a GED. And she's behaved in ways that sometimes offend the cultural sensibilities of the professional class. Recently, she was kicked out of a Denver theater for vaping, groping her male companion, and generally being disruptive.[33] Similarly, Ed Durr, a truck driver, won a state Senate seat in New Jersey. Like Boebert, Durr's conservative politics is colored by his ugly crassness. He recently came under fire from fellow Republicans for his anti-abortion views when he wrote on Facebook: "A woman does have a choice! Keep her legs closed."[34] Meanwhile, David Farnsworth, who has an associate's degree in arts and is a former crane operator, won a

---

[32] Jeffrey M. Berry and Sarah Sobieraj, *The Outrage Media: Political Opinion Media and the New Incivility* (Oxford University Press, 2016), 167–68.

[33] Nick Mordowanec, "Lauren Boebert May Have Broken the Law with Theater Fondling," *Newsweek*, September 18, 2023, https://www.newsweek.com/lauren-boebert-may-have-broken-law-theater-fondling-1827773.

[34] Matt Friedman, "South Jersey GOP Candidates Condemn Durr Social Media Posts on Abortion," *Politico*, October 12, 2023, https://www.politico.com/news/2023/10/12/new-jersey-gop-candidates-durr-abortion-00121189.

state House seat in Arizona. Farnsworth has endured real hardships: Reportedly, he was homeless for a period and battled mental illness. He overcame those obstacles to defeat Rusty Bowers, who bravely took a stand against Donald Trump, even testifying against him before the January 6th Commission.[35]

These examples are not idiosyncratic. A 2022 study of Republican state legislators confirms what we found in Wyoming. The study reveals that members with higher levels of education are less likely to affiliate with the Tea Party. Those with prior military service, meanwhile, were more likely to affiliate with it.[36] In other Western democracies, as well, the new populists come disproportionately from the working class.[37]

As the new class-based identity politics is remaking American parties, citizens' views on masculinity now track closely with partisan identity. According to a recent survey, Republican men are much more likely than Democratic men to say they feel "very masculine." Some 54 percent of Republican men say they are very manly, compared to just 33 percent of Democratic men. These differences closely track the diploma divide: While 54 percent of men with no college experience say it's important that others see them as masculine, only 38 percent of men with a college degree agree.[38] As we've argued here, these findings should not be surprising given the enduring strength of honor cultures in middle America. And they suggest that

---

[35] Bob Christie, "Farnsworth's Story of Homelessness Prompts Senate Committee Chair to Pull Kavanagh's Proposal," *Arizona Capitol Times*, January 20, 2023, https://azcapitoltimes.com/news/2023/01/20/farnsworths-story-of-homelessness-prompts-senate-committee-chair-to-pull-kavanaghs-proposal/.

[36] Stella M. Rouse et al., "Growing Tea with Subnational Roots: Tea Party Affiliation, Factionalism, and GOP Politics in State Legislatures," *American Politics Research* 50, no. 2 (2022): 242–54.

[37] See, for example, Armin Schafer, "Return with a Vengeance: Working Class Anger and the Rise of Populism," *Items*, August 8, 2017, https://items.ssrc.org/democracy-papers/return-with-a-vengeance-working-class-anger-and-the-rise-of-populism/; David Goodhart, *The Road to Somewhere: The Populist Revolt and the Future of Politics* (Hurst and Company, 2017).

[38] Daniel A. Cox et al., "Politics, Sex, and Sexuality: The Growing Gender Divide in American Life: Findings from the March 2022 American Perspectives Survey," AEI Survey Center on American Life, April 27, 2022, https://www.americansurveycenter.org/research/march-2022-aps/. Also see Sarah H. DiMuccio and Eric D. Knowles, "Precarious Manhood Predicts Support for Aggressive Policies and Politicians," *Personality and Social Psychology Bulletin* 47, no. 7 (2021): 1169–87.

as Americans become more politically polarized along these lines of social class—with Democrats associated with feminized, highly educated
professions—it will be all the more difficult for establishment Republicans in red states like Wyoming to defend their softer way of doing
politics.

In Wyoming, these vulnerabilities have necessitated an alliance with
Democrats in the statehouse, a development that shows that this class
divide runs deeper than partisanship. For all their differences, old
guard Republican legislators and their fellow Democrats are now allied
against the new conservatives. Above all, they are guardians of the civil
professional norms that have traditionally governed their institution—
and they're equally troubled by the bomb-throwing insurgents. Representative Cathy Connolly is one of a handful of Democrats in the
Wyoming House and the first openly gay politician in the state. She's
also a professor of gender studies at the University of Wyoming. One
might think these characteristics would alienate her from the Republican leadership in the House. But that isn't the case. Instead she feels
integrated into the legislature, which has historically been built around
face-to-face relationships. And Connolly shares with her Republican
allies a sharp dislike of the new conservatives. Echoing the GOP leadership, Connolly explained: "Your job is not to bash the legislature. Your
job is to do the best for the state."

These same sentiments were also expressed by Republican Tom Walters, a soft-spoken rancher from Casper who has watched the culture of
the legislature change since he first took his seat in 2013. "When I was
elected as a new member," Walters recalled, "you knew that you needed
to keep your mouth shut and do a lot more listening than speaking so
that you could learn. And the newer members do a lot more speaking and a lot less listening and learning." When they talk, moreover,
it's often to hurl insults at the leadership. "They say things about people, not issues," Walter lamented. "They step out of line, and need to be
corrected."

Walter's reverence for the statehouse is shared by the establishment
more generally. Recently the House leadership penned an editorial that
expressed their gratitude to its distinguished history. "Walking through
the hallways of the Capitol," they wrote, "we are awed by looking at the
photographs of those who have done this work for prior generations

and fully appreciative of the opportunity to do some real good for our state."[39]

* * * * *

The establishment's love for the Wyoming statehouse is mirrored in the Cheney clan's reverence for the US House of Representatives. Like Walters and other state leaders, the Cheneys have long seen themselves as reverent defenders of its more honorable traditions. The family's ties to the House begin, of course, with Dick. From 1979 to 1989 he served in the seat Liz would later hold. In those years, Cheney shared little in common with his bomb-throwing colleague Newt Gingrich, who entered the Congress in the same freshman class. Unlike Cheney, Gingrich had almost no regard for the decorous traditions of the House. As the Republican journalist Stephen Hayes described their differences: "Cheney was a strong believer in the legislative process, in bipartisan compromise, in working within the system; Gingrich preferred confrontation and wanted to bring fundamental change to the Congress by dismantling the existing power structure." Democrats who knew the House in these years agree with Hayes. Leon Panetta, former chief of staff to Bill Clinton, observed of Dick: "He always recognized the importance of the process, of getting something done, in contrast to Newt Gingrich, who stood off to the side and just threw bombs."[40]

Even after serving as the secretary of defense and two terms as vice president, Dick Cheney always felt a special affection for the House. When he left the House to serve in the Pentagon under the first President Bush, Cheney admitted that he "always felt a little sad." As Hayes noted in his biography of Cheney, "he speaks of its traditions and oddities with the peculiar reverence of a member of the club."

Cheney's service in the executive branch didn't extinguish that special feeling of fraternity. When he became vice president, Cheney was offered an office in the Senate, as is customary since veeps are

---

[39] Albert Sommers et al., "Legislative Work Reflects Wyoming Values," *Pinedale Roundup*, March 23, 2023, https://pinedaleroundup.com/article/legislative-work-reflects-wyoming-values.

[40] Hayes, *Cheney*, 160.

officially president of the Senate. However, the House speaker also offered Cheney an office in the House, which the new veep accepted.[41]

Even before Dick was elected to the House, he was fascinated by its deliberative traditions, having embarked on a dissertation on the topic years earlier. As a member of Congress, Cheney continued to work on that earlier research, which culminated in *Kings of the Hill*, a book he co-authored with his wife about the House's most famous speakers. First published in 1983, it praised these speakers for their institutional devotion to the House, despite its poor reputation in populist circles. The Cheneys wrote of America's great and otherwise motley speakers: "One characteristic they invariably shared was a love for the institution they served. The tartest-tongued of them sometimes waxed sentimental about it, and there was no surer way to provoke them than to suggest, as their countrymen all too often did, that the House was an ignoble institution."[42] *Kings of the Hill* was rightly regarded by its admirers and critics alike as a reverent history, one the *Washington Post* called "an unabashed work of love." The elder Cheneys dedicated this "work of love" to their daughters, Liz and Mary.

Thus, when Liz was first elected to the House in 2016, she was already inoculated by her parents against the new politics, which at its best treats legislatures as mere stages on which to conduct performances and at its worst sees them as corrupt citadels that should be burned to the ground. Later, when the institution that Dick wrote so lovingly about was invaded by a violent mob, Liz, like her father, stood ready to defend the Capitol against those who sought to tarnish it. Thus, Liz didn't just vote for Trump's impeachment; she also agreed to co-chair the January 6th Commission, which was tasked with investigating the insurrection against the Capitol.

When the January 6th Committee began, Liz was escorted into the House chamber by her father. When asked by a journalist why he joined her, Liz replied: "Well, he has so much tremendous love for the institution of the House, and obviously it is something that we've shared." And, so, Dick visited the House he loved for perhaps the last time.

---

[41] Hayes, *Cheney*, 308.

[42] Richard B. Cheney and Lynne V. Cheney, *Kings of the Hill: How Nine Powerful Men Changed the Course of American History* (Touchstone, 1996), xiii.

"He wanted to be here to pay his respects," Liz added. "He wanted to be here to commemorate the grave nature of what happened."[43]

Liz Cheney's love for the Congress and Trump's war to destroy it were also rooted in different class-based systems of honor. Because the Congress questioned Trump's victory—and hence his strength—he summoned an army to the Capitol's steps. Meanwhile, Liz Cheney fought for a different code of honor. Cheney is governed by what the Yale political theorist Steven Smith calls "enlightened patriotism," one that insists on "loyalty to a particular constitutional form that we call liberal democracy or constitutional democracy."[44]

Familiarity with that "constitutional form," of course, was deeply impressed upon Liz by her parents, both of whom were PhD students in political science at the University of Wisconsin and co-authored a book together on the American Congress. Liz's enlightenment is a fruit, in part, of an unusually elite education, yet another marker of a Republican war inflected by social class.

Thus, to Cheney—and many old guard Republicans in Wyoming—it would have been dishonorable to continue supporting Trump. This is why Cheney has repeatedly invoked the language of shame and honor in her war against the president. After the Capitol invasion, for example, Cheney said: "Anyone who denies the truth of what happened on January 6th ought to be ashamed of themselves."

Trump's and Cheney's rival codes of honor also incline them to think differently about political ambition. For Trump, anything that undermines his reputation as a strongman is always dishonorable. That's why he can't concede elections that he loses. Cheney's ambition, though, inclines her to care much less about the outcome of her House race, which she was willing to lose. This is because her ambition is forward-looking. She is courting the praise of future generations by making a personal political sacrifice for the public good. This is why Cheney often tells Trump apologists that "history was watching."[45]

43 "Rep. Liz Cheney Joins CNN's 'Live from the Capitol: January 6th, One Year Later,'" YouTube, 19 min., 40 sec., https://www.youtube.com/watch?v=_eqss8iFHzo.

44 Steven B. Smith, *Reclaiming Patriotism in an Age of Extremes* (Yale University Press, 2021), 158.

45 See, for example, Victoria Eavis, "Read What Rep. Liz Cheney Had to Say When She Sat Down with the Star-Tribune," *Casper Star-Tribune*, May 30, 2021,

It's not clear if Liz Cheney ever really understood the class-based honor system that shaped Trump's vendetta against her—and the cultural sensibilities of everyday Wyomingites. Unlike her father, Liz wasn't raised in Wyoming, having spent most of her childhood in the DC area. That has left her culturally removed from Wyoming's "code of the West," and thus at a disadvantage in her race against Trump's proxy candidate, Harriet Hageman.

Only her father seemed to get the problem, which is perhaps why in a last-minute TV ad Dick, cowboy hat on, challenged Trump's manhood and praised Liz's toughness. "He is a coward, a real man wouldn't lie to his supporters," Dick said. "Liz is fearless. She never backs down from a fight."[46] Dick's intervention, of course, came far too late. And probably no Republican candidate could have survived an all-out war with Trump, not in Wyoming where he is a class hero.

Whatever the case, Trump had an even harder time understanding Liz Cheney's rival system of honor. Since there are no noble defeats for Trump, Cheney's willingness to risk political death must utterly mystify him.

These rival systems of honor also help us understand why their feud was so irresolvable. Whereas even deep disagreements over policy can end in painful compromises, Cheney and Trump saw any concession in their feud as dishonorable. Trump cannot concede his 2020 election defeat, and thus Cheney could not de-escalate her war against him. They were captured by rival class-inflected codes of honor that are remaking the Republican Party.

https://trib.com/news/state-and-regional/govt-and-politics/read-what-rep-liz-cheney-had-to-say-when-she-sat-down-with-the-star/article_d229795a-81d8-5fd3-92a3-87b766a1561f.html.

[46] "Dick Cheney Brands Donald Trump 'Greatest Ever Threat to Our Republic,'" YouTube, 55 sec., https://www.youtube.com/watch?v=ro8rkZ4HQZQ.

3

Cancel Culture for Conservatives

IN 2020, A QUASI-RELIGIOUS fervor swept over our progressive college town. Suddenly, yard signs popped up, on what seemed like every block, that set forth the town's doctrinal beliefs. "In this home, we believe," the signs began, followed by a series of affirmations, like "Black lives matter," "Women's rights are human rights," "No human is illegal," and "Science is real." Such creedal professions have a long tradition in the West. The Nicene Creed, adopted in 325, begins: "We believe in one God, the Father almighty, Maker of heaven and earth, and of all things visible and invisible. And in one Lord Jesus Christ, the Son of God." This statement identified its affirmers as the true Christians, distinct from heretics. Today's progressives, like their Christian ancestors, have sometimes enforced their dogma with religious fervor, punishing and exiling anyone who doesn't conform. We have called such persecution "cancel culture."

Observers have tended to regard cancel culture as a problem that springs from left-wing identity politics, a symptom of a particular "woke" ideology.[1] The problem, however, is actually far more widespread. The new conceptions of social justice may give cancel

---

[1] See, for example, John McWhorter, *Woke Racism: How a New Religion Has Betrayed Black America* (Portfolio, 2021); Helen Pluckrose and James Lindsay, *Cynical*

culture in progressive communities some characteristic expressions, but a new, quasi-religious censoriousness is remaking the American right as well. We simply haven't noticed it as much because the American intelligentsia—conservatives included—is isolated from red-state America. What is noticeable to critics of cancel culture is its presence in the elite enclaves they know intimately, especially in journalism, Hollywood, the university, and some progressive cities.

In distant Wyoming, though, demands for adherence to a secular creed have also been a divisive and pervasive feature of Republican identity politics. For the new right, everything begins with the state party platform, which affirms: "WE believe there are Timeless Truths that will always inform and direct our party and our country regardless of current events and circumstances."[2] The platform—a series of 23 statements that melds ideals and policy—is also elaborated by a long and expanding list of party resolutions.[3] As we'll see, any departure—real or imagined—from the party's dogma can end in cancellation. Local officials have been censured. Many others have kept their heads down, hoping they won't be next. For all the complaining about wokism on the right, the Wyoming Republican Party has incubated a cancel culture as punishing as anything on the left.

This drive to punish heretics springs from the conservative identity politics outlined in the last two chapters. Since the point of politics is to demonstrate one's essence as a *true* conservative, exiling those who don't perfectly conform is a way to prove one's authenticity. It's how one practices conservatism. Thus, Wyoming's new right is as much a cousin as it is the foe of the social justice left.

This type of politics grows in homogenous communities, left and right. As Americans have sorted themselves into like-minded communities, they have created an opportunity for new insurgents to acquire

---

Theories: How Activist Scholarship Made Everything About Race, Gender, and Identity—And Why This Harms Everybody (Pitchstone Publishing, 2022); Jonathan Rauch, *The Constitution of Knowledge: A Defense of Truth* (Brookings, 2021).

[2] Wyoming Republican Party, "Platform of the Wyoming Republican Party," January 13, 2023, https://www.wyoming.gop/post/platform-of-the-wyoming-republican-party.

[3] In 2022, for example, the party passed 20 resolutions.

power by demanding greater political purity. Without the threat of enemies from the other side, it's also easier to cultivate the sense that these homogeneous spaces can and should be holy refuges, small societies uncontaminated by the rot that infects the wider society. Like their religious forebears, though, the puritans of our day still see the rot all around them. Hence, all the purges of our modern-day witches.

* * * * *

After Liz Cheney voted to impeach Donald Trump for fomenting an insurrection, the central committee of the Wyoming Republican Party sprung into action. In short order, it passed a resolution that demanded she resign from office and "immediately repay donations to her 2020 campaign" to the state party. The committee wanted Cheney to beg for mercy as well, insisting that she "explain her actions" at an upcoming meeting.[4] Left unsaid is whether this pleading should happen before or after Cheney resigned from office. Months later, another anti-Cheney censure resolution passed the central committee. This one said that Cheney is no longer recognized as a Republican.[5] In the eyes of the state party, she is not even a Republican in name only (RINO).

Unsatisfied with a mere condemnation of Liz Cheney, the party later targeted her father. Its new right members were troubled by Wyoming's federal building in Casper because it was named after Dick Cheney. Thus, in 2023, the state party's central committee passed a resolution that called for the removal of Dick Cheney's name from the building. In their view, all traces of the Cheney clan should be erased from Wyoming. In its place, the resolution recommends that the building be renamed after John Fremont, the state's first presidential candidate.[6]

---

[4] Wyoming Republican Party, "Resolution from the Central Committee of the Wyoming Republican Party—Censure of Liz Cheney," passed February 6, 2021, https://www.wyoming.gop/post/resolution-from-the-central-committee-of-the-wyoming-republican-party-censure-of-liz-cheney.

[5] Associated Press, "Wyoming GOP Votes to Stop Recognizing Cheney as a Republican," National Public Radio, November 15, 2021, https://www.npr.org/2021/11/15/1056025589/wyoming-gop-votes-to-stop-recognizing-cheney-as-a-republican.

[6] Wyoming Republican Party Central Committee, "Renaming of the Dick Cheney Building in Casper, WY," passed February 11, 2023, https://www.wyoming.gop/post/renaming-of-the-dick-cheney-building-in-casper-wy.

The Republican National Committee (RNC) followed Wyoming's lead, censuring Cheney a year after the Capitol insurrection.[7] It was not merely a symbolic rebuke. The RNC decided to "cease any and all support" for Cheney given that she was a menace not just to the party but to American democracy as well. The party's resolution concluded that Cheney's behavior "has been destructive to the institution of the U.S. House of Representatives, the Republican Party and our republic."[8]

Then, over Memorial Day weekend in 2022, Donald Trump traveled to Casper, Wyoming, to formally endorse Cheney's primary challenger, Harriet Hageman. There he warned those who gathered that the greatest danger the GOP confronts is not progressive Democrats. It's traitorous Republicans. "Worse than the terrible Democrats are the backstabbing, RINO Republicans who are helping them," Trump warned the mostly Wyoming crowd.[9] After the rally, Elisabeth "Biffy" Jackson, the chair of the Uinta County Republican Party, found that the president said "one thing" that "really resonated." "He said we don't need to worry about them Democrats." Instead, "the real threat comes from within."[10]

Trump's message hit a nerve because new right activists like Biffy Jackson had been battling so-called RINOs well before the Cheney–Trump feud erupted. Their fights had little to do with loyalty to Trump. Yes, any open disagreement with Trump can court political censure, as we'll see. But often Wyoming Republicans are censured for reasons that have nothing to do with Trump.

Websites have emerged that help the new censors identify politically incorrect Republicans. One is called WyoRINO. Its aim is to expose RINOs in the state legislature by scrutinizing their voting records for signs

[7] Sam Metz, "GOP Censures Liz Cheney and Adam Kinzinger for Participation in Jan. 6 Investigation," *PBS News Hour*, February 4, 2022, https://www.pbs.org/newshour/politics/gop-censures-liz-cheney-and-adam-kinzinger-for-participation-in-jan-6-investigation.

[8] "Read the Republican Censure of Cheney and Kinzinger," *New York Times*, February 4, 2022, https://www.nytimes.com/interactive/2022/02/04/us/rnc-resolution-censure-cheney-kinziger.html.

[9] "Former President Trump Rally for House Candidate in Wyoming," C-SPAN, May 28, 2022, https://www.c-span.org/video/?520178-1/president-trump-holds-rally-house-candidate-wyoming.

[10] Biffy Jackson, Facebook, May 29, 2022.

they are straying from the party platform and resolutions. WyoRINO warns its visitors: "One of the most concerning issues involves the on-going trend of Democrats running on the Republican ticket. It isn't any secret that the enemy from within has been savvy to this for many years—leftists successfully being elected by the unwitting, uninformed and uninvolved citizenry in Wyoming."

How big is this problem? According to WyoRINO, practically all Wyoming politicians are faking it. In 2022 it found that approximately two out of every three Republican legislators are pretenders.[11] In 2023, thanks to pressure and turnover, the numbers improved. But, over the years, these sellouts have been plentiful enough for WyoRINO to award a "RINO of the Month." As of this writing, 53 Republican legislators have received this designation since 2020, permanent members of the RINO "Hall of Shame."[12] That's a substantial number, even accounting for the fact that a few representatives have won it multiple times.

If WyoRINO is correct, that means that Wyoming—a state Gallup recently ranked as the most conservative in the union[13]—is not what it seems. It's actually governed by a dishonest clique of progressives. Actual conservatives are a minority.

WyoRINO's dragnet is so thick that even those who consider themselves to be new right legislators sometimes get caught in its netting. One such representative was John Romero-Martinez, who served in the statehouse until 2023. He is hardly an establishment Republican. Romero-Martinez is a QAnon-styled conspiracist who recently threatened the lives of a lobbyist and fellow representative because he believed they were involved in a secret pedophile ring.[14] Even so, he

---

[11] See House and Senate Scorecards for 2022, https://wyorino.com/wp-content/uploads/2022/04/2022-Senate-House-Scorecard.pdf.

[12] "RINOs Hall of Shame," https://wyorino.com/rinos-hall-of-shame/.

[13] Frank Newport, "Wyoming, North Dakota and Mississippi Most Conservative," Gallup, January 31, 2017, https://news.gallup.com/poll/203204/wyoming-north-dakota-mississippi-conservative.aspx.

[14] Jonathan Make, "Latest Allegations of Threats Among Wyoming Legislators Lead Some to Seek a Return to Civility," *Wyoming Tribune Eagle*, May 17, 2022, https://www.wyomingnews.com/news/local_news/latest-allegations-of-threats-among-wyoming-legislators-lead-some-to-seek-a-return-to-civility/article_5c7728eb-3bea-5a55-8e34-b6538857f861.html.

did hold some positions that ran afoul of the new right's orthodoxy, like support for Medicaid expansion in Wyoming. Such votes earned him a "RINO of the Month" in September 2021 and branded him as just "another phony, disingenuous politician."[15] It didn't matter that Romero-Martinez had been a leading right-to-life activist in the state legislature.[16] He needed to be placed in the "Hall of Shame."

We should stress that this site—and others like it—are well known in Wyoming. WyoRINO is advertised on billboards (see Figure 3.1). So is the new controversial site Honor Wyoming (see Figure 3.2), which has also been assisted by a well-funded social media campaign.[17] Drawing

FIGURE 3.1 WyoRINO's Billboard in Cheyenne.

---

[15] See "RINO of the Month September 2021," https://wyorino.com/rino-of-the-month-september-2021/.

[16] Sofia Jeremias, "Recent Elections, Activism Paved Way for Abortion 'Trigger' Law," WyoFile, March 17, 2022, https://wyofile.com/recent-elections-fresh-activism-paved-way-for-abortion-ban-trigger-law/.

[17] Leo Wolfson, "Murky Political Group Honor Wyoming Slowly Emerging From the Shadows," *Cowboy State Daily*, May 20, 2024.

FIGURE 3.2   Honor Wyoming's Billboard in Rock Springs.

on familiar rodeo terms and a larger set of voting data, Honor Wyoming calls good legislators "Top Hands" and brands those its regards as Republican sellouts (along with all Democrats) "Clowns." The latter, it says, have "low integrity."

Differences between the two sites demonstrate the schismatic tendency of creedal politics. They disagree on their assessments of some lawmakers. For example, while Republican representatives Ocean Andrew and Scott Heiner both boast perfect WyoRINO scores, they are besmirched with accusations of having "questionable integrity" by Honor Wyoming. Though some of its appraisals diverge from those of WyoRINO, it also stresses the importance of legislators' fidelity to the Wyoming GOP platform. And, like WyoRINO, it finds that most Republican legislators are not true conservatives.[18]

Of course, at least a few of Wyoming's legislators *are* real RINOs. In a one-party state like Wyoming, moderate and center-left candidates have a strong incentive to run as Republicans if they want to shape the state's policies. Pat Sweeney, a representative from Casper, is a good example. When we dined with him over lunch, we were surprised to

---

[18] Of the 86 elected Republicans some 49 had "low integrity" in the spring of 2024. See https://brand.honorwyoming.org/.

discover that he supports abortion rights. Sweeney also has frequently expressed other progressive enthusiasms. In 2021, for example, he sponsored a hate crime bill. (Wyoming is just one of three states without such a law.)[19]

But Sweeney is an outlier. Thus, when new insurgents like Biffy Jackson fear "the enemy within," they are not really thinking about RINOs like Sweeney, at least not primarily. They are thinking about a majority of the Republican politicians in Wyoming.

They are thinking about people like state Senator Cale Case. Senator Case was censured by the Fremont County GOP for advocating for Medicaid expansion. (Case represents Fremont County in the state legislature.) It didn't matter that polls show the resolution was probably wrong about the will of the governed since a majority of Wyoming Republicans support Medicaid expansion.[20] Nor did it matter that Case's district includes a Native American reservation, and a treaty obliges the federal government to provide its citizens with medical care. Under the new creedalism, no allowances can be made for prudential adjustments to principle.

Case had crossed a line. Voting 11–7, a majority of Fremont County's party officials passed a resolution that read: "Wyoming State Senator [Case] consistently speaks and acts in [sic] contrary to the will and consent of the governed and the Wyoming Republican party platform." Or, as one new right precinct committeeman put it, Case must be "held to account" for his transgressions. Much like their counterparts on the social justice left, activists in Wyoming's new guard see themselves as agents of moral accountability. And they tend to see a party establishment that is full of backsliding compromises. A new right activist who supported Case's censure said: "This entire country is a wreck on account of the conga line of RINO Republicans that we have in our midst."[21]

---

[19] Patrick Sweeney, "Wyoming Is Past Due for Bias-Motivated Crime Law," *Casper Star-Tribune*, May 16, 2021.

[20] American Cancer Society, "New Poll: Majority of Wyoming Voters Support Medicaid Expansion," press release, October 19, 2021, https://www.fightcancer.org/releases/new-poll-majority-wyoming-voters-support-medicaid-expansion.

[21] Maggie Mullen, "Sen. Cale Case Latest Subject of GOP Censure," WyoFile, May 12, 2022, https://wyofile.com/sen-cale-case-latest-subject-of-gop-censure/.

Wyoming's establishment Republicans disagree. One official who voted against the resolution is John Brown, a critic of the new insurgents and Cheney supporter. When we caught up with him in a Riverton diner, Brown did not mince words. "It was just stupid," he said. "The vitriol and the crap he had to take because of that just wasn't right." "For this new group," he added, "everything is important." "They're not going to cede one inch of ground over anything."

Senator Case didn't take the censure lying down either. He shot back in an editorial for the *Cowboy State Daily*: "At every turn, the Republican State Party leadership gives voice to a minority viewpoint that will not tolerate disagreement. Tactics include censure and RINO-labeling of any dissenting viewpoint."[22]

JoAnn True—a Cheney supporter who is affiliated with the Natrona County GOP—has also been censured by the state party. She provoked the party's ire after founding the Cowgirl Run Fund, a nonprofit organization that gives money to female candidates regardless of their political affiliation.[23] While the Run Fund mostly gives to candidates in nonpartisan races at the municipal level, it does support those who eventually seek higher offices. And among those who do, some run as Democrats. It was this fact that bothered new right activists, perhaps not unreasonably. Founding a political action committee (PAC) that funds even a handful of Democrats, after all, might look like betrayal.

Even if the act might be objectionable, though, the new right saw it as unforgivable. Marti Halverson, a member of the party's central committee, advocated for True's censure. True, she said, "has no place on the Central Committee of the Wyoming Republican Party and ought to step down immediately."[24] "As a Republican," Halverson explained, "I

[22] Jimmy Orr, "Cale Case: Big-Tent Republicans, We Need You," *Cowboy State Daily*, April 24, 2022, https://cowboystatedaily.com/2022/04/24/cale-case-big-tent-republicans-we-need-you/.

[23] Nick Reynolds, "Natrona County GOP Member Censured by State Party for Supporting Women's PAC," *Casper Star-Tribune*, January 27, 2021, https://trib.com/news/state-nd-regional/govt-and-politics/natrona-county-gop-member-censured-by-state-party-for-supporting-womens-pac/article_fb93e28d-e5bd-5674-aa47-b650c3156c19.html.

[24] Annaliese Wiederspahn, "Marti Halverson: Censure of Elected Republican Officer Warranted," *Cowboy State Daily*, September 18, 2020, https://cowboystatedaily.com/2020/09/18/marti-halverson-censure-of-elected-republican-officer-warranted/.

find the funding of a Democrat woman over an incumbent Republican man by a Republican woman in party leadership offensive on many levels."[25] Continuing in that same spirit, Halverson said the Run Fund was "inherently a sexist notion" since it rests on the assumption that women are more able representatives than men.[26] In Halverson's account, then, True is not only a sellout; she is also a bigot. Thus, she must be excommunicated from the GOP for her actions.

The censure came as a surprise to JoAnn True, who is no Rockefeller Republican. "I am a pro-life mom of six who worked in oil and gas for 20 years," JoAnn told us. She's also worked on several GOP campaigns. "To hear that I'm not a conservative is pretty shocking to me."

Those who criticize the new cancel culture are sometimes censured as well. Doctor Joe McGinley, a leader from Natrona County, was censured by the state party at a closed meeting he wasn't invited to attend, apparently for speaking out against the new insurgents. After the censure, McGinley received a disciplinary letter from the party that said as much: "Chairman McGinley has actively worked to undermine the Wyoming Republican Party by publicly making damaging statements to the media, discussing actions at a State Central Committee meeting that should not have been aired outside of the organization, and by active revolt against the organization."[27] In other words, McGinley is guilty of criticizing the new guard.

The same fate befell Cyrus Western, a state legislator and current house majority whip. He was censured by the Sheridan County GOP for his part in the circulation of a mailer that accused some of the new insurgents of "trying to tear our state apart." The censure campaign against Western was strengthened when it was discovered that he was associated with a PAC that was not registered with the secretary of state. But there is little doubt that the campaign against Western had

---

[25] This is the standard form that identity-based arguments take on the left. They begin by announcing an identity and then insist that others' actions or thoughts have offended it. According to political scientist Mark Lilla, they take this formulation: "Speaking as an X [who thinks A], I am offended you claim B." See Mark Lilla, *The Once and Future Liberal: After Identity Politics* (HarperCollins, 2017), 88.

[26] Wiederspahn, "Marti Halverson."

[27] Nick Reynolds, "Natrona County GOP Chair Says He Was Censured by State Party," *Casper Star-Tribune*, January 27, 2021, https://trib.com/news/state-and-regional/govt-and-politics/natrona-county-gop-chair-says-he-was-censured-by-state-party/article_782611e1-73ab-59f5-9f9d-dd134bcb2002.html.

more to do with his loyalty to Wyoming's Republican old guard. In the year prior to the censure, Western so irked the new guard that he won "RINO of the Month" *twice*.[28] When he won the second time, WyoRINO declared that all this recognition was well earned: "No politician better exemplifies Wyoming's RINO problem than the House Majority Whip himself." His noted transgressions included voting to increase education spending and workers' compensation benefits.[29]

Then, in 2024, the party's central committee voted to censure the state governor, Mark Gordon. The censure resolution condemned Gordon "in the strongest possible terms" for vetoing two bills. One bill would have repealed gun-free zones, forcing schools like the University of Wyoming to allow citizens to carry weapons on their grounds.[30] The governor objected to the bill partly for conservative reasons. As he explained in a veto letter, the bill promises to weaken "historic local control norms by giving sole authority to the Legislature to micromanage a constitutionally protected right." And while the governor pointed to his strong record of support for gun rights, he also stressed that the right is not "unlimited."[31] The second bill would have provided property tax relief. Gordon objected, though, because the bill would crater funding to schools and local governments.[32] His vote, though, suggested no general opposition to tax relief. In fact, Gordon had just signed into law three tax bills.[33]

---

[28] Joseph Beaudet, "Cyrus Western Censured by Sheridan GOP," *Casper Star-Tribune*, March 21, 2023, https://trib.com/news/state-and-regional/govt-and-politics/cyrus-western-censured-by-sheridan-gop/article_4dd201cc-c81e-11ed-9b9b-e34ce7838142.html.

[29] "RINO of the Month February 2023," https://wyorino.com/rino-of-the-month-february-2023/.

[30] Maya Shimizu Harris, "Wyoming GOP Could Censure Gordon Over Contentious Vetoes," WyoFile, April 19, 2024, https://wyofile.com/wyoming-gop-could-censure-gordon-over-contentious-vetoes/.

[31] See veto letter, https://drive.google.com/file/d/1ojbWXHVaZ795aM3TsqvYNAEov4WYabIp/view.

[32] See veto letter, https://drive.google.com/file/d/1hZ4tmzsrswW9tRtvJGiJLozWHBKwfdxR/view.

[33] Maggie Mullen, "Gordon Signs Property Tax Relief Package into Law," WyoFile, March 21, 2024, https://wyofile.com/gordon-signs-property-tax-relief-package-into-law/.

Gordon's defenses didn't persuade the new right members of the party's central committee. For them, governing doesn't involve balancing different conservative goods, like local control and personal freedom or public safety and gun rights. Nor were they willing to consider Gordon's record on tax relief in a more holistic way. For them, each veto was a violation of a sacred creed, established by the platform and the resolutions of the party. Hence, they need to be held accountable. As one new right party activist explained, these infractions show that the governor is a "Democrat disguised as a Republican." "I think he needs to be made an example of."[34]

For governing conservatives in the establishment such censures reflect a basic misunderstanding of politics. One such Republican is Tom Walters, a representative who lives on the outskirts of Casper. "You either agree or you're off the island," Walters told us in a crowded Casper diner one morning. A defender of viewpoint diversity, Walters noted: "They don't realize that there are going to be a lot of other people who don't agree. And that's okay. They are not bad people because they disagree." Finding common ground in a world of conflicting interests, he added, "is really the art of politics."

The creedalism described in this chapter isn't divorced from the class-based politics we described in Chapter 2. This is because all of the censured party leaders—Case, True, McGinley, Western, and Gordon—have something else in common: They are from Wyoming's upper class. And that makes them especially suspect in a party increasingly identified with the working class. Case has a doctorate in economics. True belongs to one of the richest and most powerful families in the state. McGinley is a Stanford-educated physician. Western earned a graduate degree at Harvard—a fact he seems to be hiding since it goes unmentioned on his government profile page. Western seems to need some cover, having married a physician who grew up summering in Southampton, New York.[35] And, finally, Gordon was educated at Middlebury, an elite liberal arts college in Vermont. His family also

---

[34] Harris, "Wyoming GOP Could Censure Gordon."

[35] Alana Tosti, "Hillary & Cyrus: Patriotic Chic," *Philadelphia Style*, January 20, 2022, https://phillystylemag.com/Hillary-Cyrus-Patriotic-Chic.

hails from old money from New England, the descendent of tycoons, industrialists, and philanthropists.

Thus, while all Republicans are expected to toe the line, those from privileged backgrounds are subjected to special scrutiny. As Jesus told his disciples: "It is easier for a camel to go through the eye of a needle, than for a rich man to enter into the Kingdom of God."[36] It's not quite as difficult for members of Wyoming's upper crust to enter the good graces of the new right. Their margins for error are just thinner.

In this respect, too, new right politics resembles identity politics on the left more than many have recognized. Like their progressive counterparts, all of these censures of privileged Republican elites invert a long-standing social hierarchy. None of this is exactly new, either. There is also a longer history of class-inflected social revenge on the American populist right. In *Beyond the Melting Pot*, Nathan Glazer and Patrick Moynihan suggested that Irish Catholics were drawn to the anti-communist crusade partly because it elevated their social status, particularly vis-à-vis, privileged WASPs, who were increasingly objects of suspicion.[37]

And like the liberal establishment in progressive places, Wyoming's old right worries that the larger problem with these censures is the culture of fear it cultivates. After all, no one wants to be labeled a liberal, a Democratic, or a sellout. One Republican lawmaker only admitted sotto voce to being a "moderate," despite the fact that the coffee shop where we met was deserted. Some critics of the new right are certainly keeping their heads down. After Liz Cheney became a lightning rod in the state for opposing Trump, a private Facebook group of local politicos who support her was created. It's a "safe space of support," one establishment legislator told us.

There are outspoken exceptions, of course. One is Landon Brown, an old guard legislator from Cheyenne. Brown embraces the RINO label as a badge of honor, sporting a lapel pin of a rhino in the statehouse. He also openly supported Cheney. "As far as I'm aware, I'm the only

---

[36] Mark 10:25.

[37] Nathan Glazer and Patrick P. Moynihan, *Beyond the Melting Pot: The Negros, Puerto Ricans, Jews, Italians and Irish of New York City*, 2nd ed. (MIT Press, 1970), 268–72.

elected individual in the state of Wyoming that has come out in support of Liz." This is so even though Brown noted that there was "a lot of quiet support" for Liz, predicting that about half of the legislators voted for her. At times, though, Brown wonders if he has been too outspoken. "There is a portion of me that wonders if I should shut my mouth and do the same thing."

Ordinary Republicans who supported Cheney were also reluctant to speak up. In remote Fremont County, John Brown told us that it was hard to assess Cheney support among his neighbors. "There definitely is pressure to conform," he observed. "There are some more independent thinkers [locally], but unfortunately they seem to be silent." Some scattered evidence is consistent with Brown's report. One Wyoming couple, for example, assessed their own personal security risks before putting a Cheney sign up in their yard.[38]

The new climate has also made it increasingly difficult to recruit civically minded small business owners into the party, the sort who traditionally brought a pragmatic sensibility into Wyoming politics. JoAnn True, who busily tries to recruit such people for precinct positions in the Natrona County GOP, notices their reluctance. They tell her: "Everyone buys my pizzas, so I don't want to take a position." "I hear this all the time." Perhaps it's best to stay out of the firing line, if one can. Democrats, meanwhile, also notice the change and complain about the new climate of fear. One Democratic organizer observed: "There is a palpable fear of even letting your friends know you are a Democrat, or even in line with what Democratic politicians are doing."[39]

In their defense, new right activists say that complaints about the changing speech climate are disingenuous. Douglas Gerard spends much of his time identifying fake conservatives through a site that rivals WyoRINO and Honor Wyoming. He believes that "complaints about incivility or a hostile political tone often stem not from a place of reasoned debate but from frustration over losing ground in the political landscape." "Politics," he adds, is "a field of robust debate and strong

---

[38] Katty Kay, Twitter, June 15, 2022, https://twitter.com/kattykay_/status/1537128625497116674.

[39] Peder Schaefer, "'A Palpable Fear of Even Letting Your Friends Know You Are a Democrat,'" *Politico*, February 7, 2024, https://www.politico.com/news/magazine/2024/02/07/democrat-rural-america-struggles-qa-00139921.

opinions."[40] Biffy Jackson, former Unita County Party chair, laughed dryly when asked about the tenor of politics. She found it frustrating that citizens would vote for candidates whom she deems RINOs simply because they are "nice." Furthermore, she denied her faction was the source of the problem: "I'm extreme. I'll admit it. It's fine. [But] I have never once called somebody a name. I've never once yelled at somebody. I've never once punched somebody in the face." "We're not the ones doing that, they are," Biff continued. "It's the more moderate RINOs . . . accusing us of things we are not doing. They are the ones physically assaulting people. They are the ones suing every fifteen minutes. But then they accuse us of being combative and disrespectful."

It's also important not to overstate the climate of fear. This is so partly because speech climates are not the same everywhere, even within the state party. The Republican establishment has retained smaller—but significant—bastions of power. One is the Natrona County GOP, which remains a refuge and a center of establishment power. On a cold February evening in 2022 it held its annual Lincoln Day Dinner, attended by many anti-MAGA Republicans, including Liz Cheney. The keynote address was given by Wyoming's elder statesperson, Al Simpson. A beloved figure in the state, Simpson served in the US Senate for 18 years and in the statehouse before that. Now in his 90s, Simpsons can still deliver a speech that endeared him to so many Wyomingites.

Never one to mince words, Simpson didn't go after the Biden administration that evening or the Alexandria Ocasio-Cortez wing of the Democratic Party. Instead, he waded into Wyoming's Republican civil war by criticizing the new censorious culture that has swept over the state party. Simpson especially criticized his fellow Republicans for labeling everyone they disagree with a RINO, offering his own definition of those who use the term: "Republicans Irritatingly and Ignorantly Needling Others." The line got a big laugh.

* * * * *

---

[40] Evidence Based Wyoming, "Rating the Raters: Unmasking WYCAP's 'Conservative' Scores—A Tale of Transparency, Twists, and Tenuous Truths," November 19, 2023, https://evidencebasedwyoming.com/2023/11/19/rating-the-raters-unmasking-wycaps-conservative-scores-a-tale-of-transparency-twists-and-tenuous-truths/?doing_wp_cron=1717936772.8083629608154296875000.

The state party is an institution ideally suited for practitioners of a creedal, identity politics. Not only is it in control of the institution but most of its actions consist in passing resolutions and censures. In its committee meetings, activists spend hours parsing language. Like the social justice activists on the left, words are even parsed to expose their insidious implications. We observed a delegate at the state convention argue that Wyoming schoolchildren should not be required to say the pledge of allegiance since the word "indivisible" suggests that states can't secede from the union.[41]

In the legislature, though, the new right faces bigger challenges practicing its creedal politics. Unlike the state party, old guard Republicans have maintained control of the state legislature—and they tend to focus on more technocratic policies and concerns. New guard types also face a challenge some didn't anticipate: Wyoming's laws already rank among the most conservative in the nation. Compared to other states, Wyoming has the second lowest tax burden, and it has some of the weakest gun control laws.[42] In fact, it is *the best state* in the union for gun enthusiasts, according to a ranking by *Guns and Ammo* magazine.[43] Thus, there is already a lot of symmetry between the conservative creed—elaborated in the party platform and resolutions—and state law.

Under those conditions, how does the new right carve out a legislative agenda?

---

[41] While the party didn't ultimately adopt that position, it wasn't because there isn't real support for succession in the state party leadership. The chair of the Wyoming Republican Party, Frank Eathorne, has suggested that the state should secede from the union. He was also on the Capitol grounds during the January 6th invasion.Victoria Eavis and Rone Tempest, "Wyoming GOP Chairman Quietly Assumed Power as Party Fractured," WyoFile, May 20, 2022, https://trib.com/news/state-and-regional/govt-and-politics/wyo-gop-chairman-quietly-assumed-power-as-party-fractured/article_462b1378-d7c4-11ec-9d00-97f1199ecd2b.html.

[42] Erica York and Jared Walczak, "State and Local Tax Burdens, Calendar Year 2022," Tax Foundation, April 7, 2022, https://taxfoundation.org/publications/state-local-tax-burden-rankings/; Giffords Law Center, "Annual Gun Law Scorecard," https://giffords.org/lawcenter/resources/scorecard/.

[43] Keith Woods, "The Best States for Gun Owners: Ranked for 2022," *Guns and Ammo*, August 18, 2022, https://www.gunsandammo.com/editorial/best-states-for-gun-owners-2022/463592.

One strategy is to insist, contrary to the weight of the evidence, that moral contamination is everywhere. Just as progressive activists in American colleges and universities insist that some of the least racist institutions in the United States are plagued by racism, new right legislators in Wyoming see critical race theory in its schools. And, so, in 2022 they sponsored a bill that prohibited the teaching of critical race theory in Wyoming public schools.[44] It didn't pass because old-line conservatives don't think it's a real problem.

New right legislators should also know that there isn't much anti-Republican election fraud happening in Wyoming, not in a state where the vast majority of county clerks are Republicans. Yet some groups are even advocating for a return to hand-counted ballots because they don't trust the state's voting machines. Thus, in a state where Trump won 70 percent of the vote, MAGA sympathizers fear its elections are somehow rigged.

The problem was severe enough that Wyoming's former secretary of state, Ed Buchanan, hit the road. Buchanan developed a PowerPoint presentation he showed to voters around the state in an effort to convince them that Wyoming's elections are secure.[45] In the legislature, though, some new right lawmakers still suggested otherwise. Thus, they passed an election integrity bill, one that required citizens to present identification before voting. As an annoyed and somewhat bemused Democratic representative told us: "There is no solution to a non-problem."

Another way new right lawmakers pursue a legislative agenda is by finding new ways to signal the state's fidelity to conservative principles, especially on culture war issues. Wyoming's gun laws, for example, are some of the most permissive in the nation. Any Wyoming citizen can open-carry practically anywhere they please, without a permit or license. Exemptions include schools and government buildings. So, new

---

[44] See State of Wyoming—68th Legislature, "HB0097—Ban on Teaching and Training Critical Race Theory," https://www.wyoleg.gov/Legislation/2022/HB0097.

[45] Amanda Fehring, "Buchanan Presented About Election Security, Integrity in Lander Tuesday," *County 10*, June 9, 2022, https://county10.com/buchanan-presented-about-election-security-integrity-in-lander-tuesday/.

right legislators pushed a bill to remove those limited restrictions.[46] More recently, the legislature passed a law that requires local law enforcement officials to ignore any future federal law that violates the Second Amendment. Violators are subject to a year in prison and a $2,000 dollar fine.[47]

For governing conservatives, the problem with the new right's legislative agenda is that it wastes too much time on laws that are either fanciful (like bans on critical race theory) or imprudent (like the gun bill), which distract the legislature from more pressing problems.

Time is an especially valuable resource in a citizen legislature like Wyoming's, which meets for only a few months every year. As JoAnn True lamented: "We spend such an inordinate amount of time, especially in the legislature, talking about guns and abortion and gender issues." Representative Cathy Connolly, one of just five Democratic representatives in the statehouse, felt these time pressures keenly: "Because of these things and because of their traction, we spend time on them. And, again, we have very limited time. Very limited time." Bigger problems get slighted. "We have one of the highest suicide rates in the nation," she told us, grimly. "We now have the highest workplace fatality rate. We've got COVID issues. We've got hospitals closing. We're not looking at these issues because we have these stupid ass bills."

Of course, there is nothing wrong with bringing cultural or moral issues into our politics. There is a long and troubled philosophical tradition—extending back to James Madison—that suggests that economic interests should ideally be at the center of American politics

---

[46] Brendan Lachance, "Wyoming Again Seeing Effort to Repeal Gun Free Zones, Allow Conceal Carry at Colleges and UW," *Oil City News*, February 8, 2021, https://oilcity.news/wyoming/legislature/2021/02/08/wyoming-again-seeing-effort-to-repeal-gun-free-zones-allow-conceal-carry-at-colleges-and-uw-2/#:~:text=%E2%80%94%20Some%20Wyoming%20legislators%20are%20again,legislature's%202020%20session%2C%20but%20Rep.

[47] Jasmine Hall, "Gordon Signs Second Amendment Protection Bill," *Casper Star-Tribune*, May 22, 2022, https://trib.com/news/state-and-regional/govt-and-politics/gordon-signs-second-amendment-protection-bill/article_5724f75c-d04a-5d41-b11a-787d4ddbf1b9.html.

because they are somehow more reasonable and weighty than other kinds of claims.[48]

The view is mistaken. There have been plenty of serious and thoughtful moral crusaders in the modern right. The pro-life movement, for example, has long made serious claims about the nature of basic human rights and mostly framed them in secular terms.[49] Right or wrong, it's a cause that some voters reasonably care more about than, say, the distribution of local liquor licenses or the marginal tax rate. Likewise, the gun issue is understandably an important one to citizens in a state like Wyoming where even the Democrats pack heat.

The problem with the new right in Wyoming is not that it cares about these issues; it's that it keeps waging wars it has already won.

* * * * *

Although the new right's creedal identity politics—and the cancel culture it cultivated—resembles the left's in many respects, there is one major difference: Donald Trump. Its seeds, though, were planted well before Trump rose to power. They developed during the Obama era, when the Tea Party rose to power. From the beginning, Tea Party activists distrusted the GOP establishment's commitment to conservative principles. Many of its one-time champions were pushed out of the party for their perceived moderation, including Eric Cantor and John Boehner.[50] In this era, talk radio and Fox News increasingly policed Republican politicians. "If you stray the slightest from the far right, you get hit by the conservative media," former US senator Trent Lott lamented.[51] And contrary to some accounts, the Tea Party didn't die. It simply took over many local and state parties, a perch from which it

---

[48] Jon A. Shields, *The Democratic Virtues of the Christian Right* (Princeton University Press, 2009), 6–10, 147–59.

[49] Shields, *Democratic Virtues of the Christian Right*, 33–39; see also Jon A. Shields, "The Politics of Motherhood Revisited," *Contemporary Sociology* 41, no. 1 (2012): 43–48.

[50] Rachel B. Blum, *How the Tea Party Captured the GOP* (University of Chicago Press, 2020), 8, 27, 31–32, 35, 40–41, 44, 72–73, 78; Theda Skocpol and Vanessa Williamson, *The Tea Party and the Remaking of Republican Conservatism* (Oxford University Press, 2012), 27, 89.

[51] Steven Levitsky and Daniel Ziblatt, *How Democracies Die* (Crown, 2019), 223; See also Jeffrey M. Berry and Sarah Sobieraj, *The Outrage Media: Public Opinion, Media, and the New Incivility* (Oxford University Press, 2014), 180, 189–90, 223.

could monitor and cajole party regulars in the legislature. It also made inroads into many state legislatures.[52] In these respects, Wyoming is typical of other states where the Tea Party was strong.

Trump did change conservative cancel culture, though. He did so by wedding the new politics of identity to a personality cult and a campaign to steal an election, making it more dangerous than its rival on the left. "He just poured gasoline on everything that was going on in the state," JoAnn True told us. "It became very much a division. Do you support him? Do you not support him? And that became very much a litmus test." Gail Symons, a longtime GOP activist who ran for the statehouse unsuccessfully, is also dismayed by these changes. Now, she says, it's not acceptable to say "anything" bad about Trump, adding: "This is scary shit. This is China! This is authoritarian." "This is not the party I joined 48 years ago."

Opposition to Cheney highlights these changes well. Her voting record did not deviate sharply from Trump's positions, and where it did, it was mostly due to her own greater fidelity to conservative principles. Yet Cheney is not only considered a RINO by many Wyoming Republicans—she has been made into the face of greater RINO-dom. Tim Lasseter, president of Park County Right to Life, sported a T-shirt at the state party convention that said "No More RINOs" with Cheney's name circled and crossed out.[53]

Harriet Hageman, meanwhile, repeatedly berated Cheney for failing to represent Wyoming's "values." But in truth Cheney is considered the mother of all RINOs for reasons that have nothing to do with conservative values. After all, Cheney doesn't have many ideological disagreements with the new right or Hageman. She just opposes Trump.

For some Wyomingites, Trump has become the party, a fact that troubles many old-line Republicans in the state. As one Cheyenne-based politico from Cheney's clique, who preferred to remain anonymous, told us: "Trump has completely rewritten the word conservative; now, all it means is how loyal are you to Trump." Gail

[52] Skocpol and Williamson, *Tea Party*, 180–83.

[53] Victoria Eavis, "Laramie County Delegates Walk Out After Losing Delegates at GOP Convention," *Casper Star-Tribune*, May 7, 2022, https://trib.com/news/state-and-regional/govt-and-politics/watch-now-laramie-county-republicans-walk-out-after-losing-delegates-at-gop-convention/article_4de493b0-ce31-11ec-a3c5-6b7f2d93c1fa.html#tracking-source=most-popular-homepage.

Symons agreed: "You have to say Trump is the GOP." The confusion of Trump with the GOP, and even the nation itself, was evident at a committee session to discuss party resolutions at the 2022 GOP state convention. As the committee discussed whether to issue a *third* denunciation of the congresswoman, one delegate stood up to suggest a resolution that echoed Trump's reality show, *The Apprentice*: "Cheney, You're Fired!" While the delegates debated, and ultimately rejected, additional censures, one long-bearded, middle-aged man next to us whispered angrily under his breath, "She's a traitor."

The conflation of conservatism with Trumpism cost Cheney her leadership position in the House as well. After she was stripped of her position as party chair, Jeff Duncan (R-South Carolina) lamented that Cheney "did have a conservative record" prior to her opposition to Trump.[54] In that moment of candor, Duncan acknowledged that the decision to remove Cheney was not just a practical one to appease angry constituents or maintain a united front. Something more fundamental had taken place: The measure of a conservative is one's loyalty to Donald Trump.

Partly for that reason, Wyoming is not the only state plagued by the new conservative cancel culture. In Colorado, the state party assesses candidates' fidelity to Trump before offering them an endorsement. In fact, those seeking an endorsement must say whether they "denounce" Americans for Prosperity, which supported Nikki Haley's bid to defeat Trump in the 2024 primary.[55] More commonly, state- and county-level parties have passed censure resolutions against GOP officials who broke with Trump.[56] Senator Bill Cassidy, for example, was censured by his hometown county in Louisiana for voting for Trump's impeachment after January 6th. "We condemn Senator Cassidy's actions in the strongest manner," the resolution declared. "He does not represent the people of

54 Robert Draper, "Liz Cheney vs. MAGA," *New York Times*, April 22, 2021, https://www.nytimes.com/2021/04/22/magazine/liz-cheney-vs-maga.html?referringSource=articleShare.

55 Michelle Goldberg, "The Gay-Bashing Email Splitting Colorado's Republican Party," *New York Times*, June 10, 2024.

56 Perry Bacon, Jr., "The Trumpiest Republicans Are at the State and Local Level—Not in DC," *FiveThirtyEight*, February 16, 2021, https://fivethirtyeight.com/features/the-trumpiest-republicans-are-at-the-state-and-local-levels-not-in-d-c/.

this state or the Republican Party."[57] Three days later the state party censured Cassidy as well.[58]

The Arizona GOP, meanwhile, censured its governor Doug Ducey and former senator Jeff Flake for their opposition to Trump. After his powerful testimony before the January 6th committee, Rusty Bowers was censured as well despite his long distinguished service in the Arizona House of Representatives. After the censure passed, Arizona's party chair tweeted: Bowers "is no longer a Republican in good standing & we call on Republicans to replace him at the ballot box in the August primary." Bowers had to be cast out. And he ultimately was. In the 2022 primary Bowers was defeated by a working-class Trumpist.[59]

As in Wyoming, Arizona's Republican Party also went after its own political royalty when it censured Cindy McCain, the widow of Senator John McCain.[60] Apparently no latitude was granted to Cindy in light of Trump's harsh words toward her husband. "He's not a war hero," Trump once said of McCain. "He was a war hero because he was captured. I like people who weren't captured."[61] McCain had been a captive for 5 and a half years in a North Vietnamese camp, enduring

[57] Republican Party of East Baton Rouge Parish, "The Censure of Senator Bill Cassidy Unanimously Adopted," Facebook, February 10, 2021, https://www.facebook.com/permalink.php?story_fbid=3841765612527752&id=289561774414838&__cft__[0]=AZV5w-SeGdSDs7p5lZXzdjkdpniXzV4SZhKWkDoVZA8vqW2uvMvE3pVSnTjBS6PAsncS9utBnaaog1jX3r4DYoinldu-HXpnScax5iLk2oLwhGDuobGRSxogfH8IuPM8fedKyDM23vR5udWkWEaojNQ-&__tn__=%2CO%2CP-R.

[58] Republican Party of Louisiana, "Official: The LAGOP Executive Committee Unanimously Votes to Censure Senator Bill Cassidy," press release, February 13, 2021, accessed May 17, 2021, https://www.lagop.com/post/official-the-lagop-executive-committee-votes-to-censure-senator-bill-cassidy.

[59] Jonathan J. Cooper, "Arizona Censures Rusty Bowers After Jan. 6 Testimony," Associated Press, July 20, 2022, https://apnews.com/article/2022-midterm-elections-capitol-siege-donald-trump-presidential-censures-f8892631bd14e1b2266af4c9d00f6af8.

[60] Matthew S. Schwartz and Emma Bowman, "Arizona Republicans Censure Party Leaders at Odds With Trump," National Public Radio, January 23, 2021, https://www.npr.org/2021/01/23/959974795/arizona-republicans-censure-party-leaders-at-odds-with-trump.

[61] Ben Schreckinger, "Trump Attacks McCain: 'I Like People Who Weren't Captured,'" Politico, July 18, 2015, https://www.politico.com/story/2015/07/trump-attacks-mccain-i-like-people-who-werent-captured-120317.

torture and grievous injuries. He heroically had refused an offer of early release, proffered to destroy the morale of remaining prisoners and to influence his father, senior commander of US forces in the Pacific in 1968.[62]

With no state-level politicians to censure, the GOP in Oregon decided to pass a resolution condemning all House Republicans who voted for Trump's impeachment. It said that these members were modern-day Benedict Arnolds since they were "conspiring to surrender our nation to Leftist forces seeking to establish a dictatorship."[63]

All of these censures by Trump loyalists caught the attention of political scientist Seth Masket. Based on a survey of local newspapers, Masket finds that some 23 Republican officeholders were censured by county-level parties in 2021, up from a combined 6 censures over the previous 5 years. The figure is an undercount of all censures since it just looks at county-level parties and only at elected officials. And it doesn't count cases—like one in Iowa—where party leaders were not formally censured but were forced to resign for criticizing Trump after the 2020 election.[64] What the data does show, though, is what Masket says is "a growing form of radicalism among local party committees."[65]

The seeds of this radicalism, though, were not planted on January 6th. In 2017, for example, Joe Straus, the speaker of the Texas House, was censured for opposing mostly symbolic bills, such as one that would restrict the public restrooms trans people can use. Like the old guard

---

[62] Philip Carter, "The Courage to Stand While Trembling," *Slate*, August 26, 2018, https://slate.com/news-and-politics/2018/08/john-mccains-unique-vietnam-war-heroism-empowered-him-in-politics.html.

[63] "Resolution of the Oregon Republican Party Condemning the Betrayal by the Ten House Republicans Who Voted to Impeach President Trump," https://www.scribd.com/document/491311574/Resolution-of-the-Oregon-Republican-Party-Condemning-the-Betrayal-by-the-Ten-House-Republicans-Who-Voted-to-Impeach-President-Trump#from_embed.

[64] Shelby Kluver, "Former Scott County GOP Chair Forced Out, Says He Still Stands by His Party," WQAD, February 8, 2021, https://www.wqad.com/article/news/politics/former-scott-county-gop-chair-forced-out/526-7e7b1ffc-f292-40aa-b4be-165891 0cb3ff.

[65] Seth Masket, "How an Uptick in Censures Among Local Republicans Signals a Growing Radicalism," *FiveThirtyEight*, March 14, 2022, https://fivethirtyeight.com/features/how-an-uptick-in-censures-among-local-republicans-signals-a-growing-radicalism/.

in Wyoming, he believes these bills are a distraction from real governing, stating that "responsible" Texas politicians should "care most about what's good for Texas." In other words, questions of mostly symbolic importance should not be central to the state party's legislative agenda.[66]

And as in Wyoming, websites are popping up in other states to help new censors identify the true, creedal conservatives. A South Dakota cite, Citizens for Liberty, gives most Republicans in its state legislature failing marks.[67] It has fueled factional wars in the state, which have grown increasingly bitter.[68] Similarly, a site in Montana separates "loyal Republicans" from "RINOs."[69] New right activists in red states like Idaho, Oklahoma, and Texas are pushing related sites.[70]

Censures also seem to be increasing in the Democratic Party. There were five in 2021, even though there were none the previous 5 years.[71] Even so, the partisan difference is striking, particularly given how prominent cancel culture has been on the inside of progressive universities and newsrooms. And the disparity can't be fully explained by conservative feuds over Trump. In 2021, Republican county organizations censured 11 elected officials for reasons unrelated to Trump's impeachment or the outcome of the 2020 election—more than twice the number of Democrats censured.

* * * * *

The new censoriousness on the right represents a sharp break from a party that has long tolerated sharp differences of opinion. As late as

---

[66] Allie Morris, "Bexar County GOP Censures House Speaker Straus," *San Antonio Express-News*, December 12, 2017, https://www.mysanantonio.com/news/local/article/Straus-censured-by-Bexar-County-GOP-12425417.php.

[67] See South Dakota Citizens for Liberty scorecard, https://www.sdcitizensforliberty.org/wp-content/uploads/2024/04/SDCFL-2024-Scorecard.pdf.

[68] Joshua Haiar, "Republican Factions Fighting for Control of the Party in Tuesday's Primary Election," *South Dakota Searchlight*, June 1, 2024, https://southdakotasearchlight.com/2024/06/01/republican-factions-fighting-for-control-of-the-party-in-tuesdays-primary-election/

[69] See https://www.legislatorloyalty.com/.

[70] They include the "Oklahoma Conservative Index," "The Texas RINO Roundup," and Idaho's "Freedom Index."

[71] Masket, "How an Uptick in Censures."

2008, the GOP presidential primaries boasted a hawk (John McCain) and an isolationist (Ron Paul), not to mention a pro-choice candidate (Rudy Giuliani). Although the GOP has long been more cohesive ideologically than Democrats, it also had to manage different issue priorities, particularly among elites. Until the Trump era, the party's establishment included an uneasy coalition of religious conservatives, foreign policy hawks, pro-business conservatives, and America-first populists. And while those elites often fought for influence inside the party, they also tolerated one another and sought common ground. Since the 1990s, these varied interests have met every week in DC to work through their differences. The meeting is so diverse it has been likened to a "*Star Wars* bar."[72]

In Wyoming these differences have traditionally been worked out in actual bars, far from the formality of the legislature. These party traditions—in both DC and Wyoming—continue, but their power to shape the culture of the larger party has waned. And, of course, the insularity of these closed gatherings has something to do with the new populism that is remaking the party.

The next chapter will show that the right's new creedalism is driven by national causes. It has, therefore, been an important agent of the nationalization of Wyoming politics and drawn it into deeper conflict with establishment Republicans who remain largely focused on local issues and concerns.

---

[72] Tom Hamburger and Peter Wallsten, *One Party County: The Republican Plan for Dominance in the 21st Century* (John Wiley & Sons, 2006), 23.

4

━━━◦◦◦━━━

National Conservatism

NOT LONG AGO, IT WASN'T very expensive to run for Congress in Wyoming. Prior to her crusade against Donald Trump, Liz Cheney typically raised a few hundred thousand dollars every quarter, mostly from Wyomingites. But that all changed after January 6th. During the first quarter of 2021 Cheney raised $1.5 million, most of it from out of state. By the spring of 2022 she had nearly $7 million for her primary contest. Her main rival, Harriet Hageman, raised millions as well, mostly from out-of-state MAGA donors.[1]

While the race stood out as one of the most expensive in the nation, it was part of a trend. Our politics is becoming increasingly nationalized. Signs of it are everywhere. Voters are less likely to know the name of their governor than they once did, and they are less likely to consume local news and to turn out in local elections. State party platforms,

---

[1] Ryan Lizza and Eugene Daniels, "Liz Cheney's Record Fundraising Haul," *Politico*, April 11, 2022, https://www.politico.com/newsletters/playbook/2022/04/11/scoop-liz-cheneys-record-fundraising-haul-00024356; Leo Wolfson, "Cheney Beats Hageman for Out-of-State $$, Hageman Beats Cheney for In State $$, Bouchard Trails," Cowboy State Daily, July 12, 2022," https://cowboystatedaily.com/2022/07/19/cheney-beats-hageman-for-out-of-state-hageman-beats-cheney-in-state-bouchard-disappears/.

meanwhile, look more alike today, making it harder for parties to maintain local brands.[2] Like our commercial strips, which are crowded with the same box stores and restaurant chains, so too do our political parties look increasingly alike, offering the same product from San Diego, California, to Bangor, Maine.

Congressional races have been no exception to what political scientist Daniel Hopkins calls our "increasingly United States." As recently as 1990 less than a third of money raised by House and Senate candidates came from out of state; by 2012, about two-thirds were raised from out-of-state contributions. And many of these come from the same handful of well-educated, affluent communities.[3]

The American right has been at the forefront of nationalizing our politics. From the Republican revolution in 1994 to the Tea Party in 2010, populist Republicans have sought to unify local House and Senate races around a common mission. These efforts have been aided by national media personalities from Rush Limbaugh to Sean Hannity. And they have paid off. As Hopkins observes, "the nationalization of vote choice" has favored Republicans, especially for legislative races in statehouses and the Congress.[4]

Even so, deep red Wyoming had long resisted these trends. It was a small place, which allowed a more parochial, face-to-face politics to thrive. From that insulation Wyoming's Republican establishment grew its own indigenous brand of politics, one that gave pride of place to those with deep roots in the state and distrusted outsiders. That parochialism also meant that national issues had no place on the state legislative agenda. Instead, the establishment catered to its big energy industries and kept taxes low but did so without forgoing a sense of noblesse oblige toward the less advantaged.

That world has been cratered by new right insurgents from the MAGA-verse who are concerned almost entirely with national causes and symbols. They have sought to send money to Texas so that it can build a border wall, passed election integrity bills, and pushed symbolic

[2] Daniel J. Hopkins, *The Increasingly United States: How and Why American Political Behavior Nationalized* (University of Chicago Press, 2018), 61, 144, 159, 197.

[3] Hopkins, *Increasingly United States*, 61, 76–77.

[4] Hopkins, *Increasingly United States*, 56.

Second Amendment laws. This makes sense given that their political world is centered in the new social media and national personalities, rather than the friends-and-neighbors politics that shaped the old party. Hence, the creedalism we described in the previous chapter has a distinctly national cast. And its national character links Wyoming's new right to similar insurgencies in other red states.

These changes raise questions about what "national conservatism" actually is. Ever since Trump pushed new concerns to the forefront of the Republican agenda, especially economic protectionism and immigration restriction, intellectuals have tried to refound the party around something that goes by the name of "national conservatism." Propagated by groups like the Edmund Burke Foundation, this national conservatism ostensibly seeks to defend America's unique traditions and character against the homogenizing effects of our increasingly global economy. Yet in practice the nationalization of American conservatism has done the opposite: It aims to destroy a rich tradition of civic localism, one that seeks to remake the party everywhere into the same basic product.

One establishment figure who has accelerated these changes is Cheney herself. While Cheney has bravely crusaded against the party of Trump, in doing so she also dramatically nationalized Wyoming politics by turning what would have been a sleepy primary contest into ground zero in the broader war over the party's future. A remarkable 95 percent of the money she raised for the race came from out of state. In these respects the Cheney–Hageman race obscures an important irony. If Wyoming's establishment wins its war with the MAGA-styled insurgents, it will be because it defeats something Cheney accelerated: the nationalization of state politics.

* * * * *

We sat down with Tim and Susan Stubson one evening at the Fire-Rock Steakhouse, a popular, upscale restaurant in Casper. They are both close to Cheney and have spent years toiling away in Wyoming politics. Looking around the steakhouse, Susan said: "In this room right now, I probably know at least four tables. I can tell you who has had COVID, who has had some deaths, whose kids are sucking it up in school." "But even if you go to Gillette or Riverton," Tim chimed in, "you are going to run into somebody you know. There is one degree of separation."

It is easy to run into politicians in Wyoming. When one of us (Muravchik) got a little disoriented heading back to our hotel room after a long day at the state convention, a kind local, who happened to be waiting for someone, steered us in the correct direction. That friendly stranger turned out to be the governor, Mark Gordon. Such experiences, we're told, are not uncommon.

For this reason, Wyoming is sometimes described by old guard Republicans as a small town with long streets. It captures Wyomingites' sense of belonging and neighborliness despite the vast stretches of land that separate them. One Republican political consultant captured the same idea when he called Wyoming "the largest small town you'll ever find."[5] Party conventions once brought these far-flung neighbors together in one spot every year. "It had a family reunion feel to it," recalled JoAnn True, a patron and party activist of the old guard. Republican politics, then, was an important source of community.

That sense of family has long been intensified by the deep roots many Republican leaders have in the state. The old guard is still led by many leaders whose parents and grandparents served in Wyoming politics. Such deep roots have traditionally been an advantage in politics since locals tend to make a sharp distinction between genuine Wyomingites and recent arrivals. Every candidate who can touts their lineage in the state. Many of our interviewees—activist, candidate, or incumbent— let us know early in our conversations how many generations back they could trace their Wyoming roots.

As many told us, one can live in the state for decades and still not really be considered a genuine Wyomingite by the locals. One local activists put it best when she told us that "you have to have sprung from the dirt" to say you are from Wyoming. She herself had been in the state 25 years, not enough time to be considered a true local, at least by some Wyomingites.

This attitude aggravates residents who were not born in the state but believe they have a right and duty to be civically engaged. Biffy Jackson, a new guard activist and former chair of the Uinta County GOP, complained that her family "moved here when I was 16. I've been here for 18 years. At what point do I become from Wyoming?! I have lived

---

5 Simone Pathé, "The Return of Liz Cheney," *Roll Call*, August 11, 2016, https:// rollcall.com/2016/08/11/the-return-of-liz-cheney/.

here a majority of my life." Her critics "assume they know more about Wyoming and Wyoming politics because they have lived here for five generations. OK," she tells her imaginary interlocutors, "but you have never been involved before. I've been doing this for 12 years. I can tell you the majority of the legislators by name and I can tell you their voting record off the top of my head. But that doesn't matter because I wasn't born here!"

Frustration with this attitude is bipartisan. When Jenefer Pasqua, an activist in her local Democratic Party, ran for the Wyoming House in Cheyenne, she quickly discovered that her neighbors wanted to know more than her party affiliation and policy positions. They wanted to know how long she had lived in the state. Jenefer wasn't a recent arrival; she has lived in Wyoming for 30 years, most of her life. But it didn't impress her neighbors. And it was no match for the "good old boy" she ran against, who proudly tells his constituents that he's a fifth-generation Wyomingite. "That was pretty disheartening," Jenefer recalled.

While those prejudices can alienate "newcomers" like Jenefer from Wyoming politics, the familialism of state politics simultaneously brings everyone close together. One transplant from New York City and activist in the party's new right marveled at the difference between political life in the Big Apple and his new home. "I met the governor!," he told us with relish. "If this was New York, I'd be lucky to meet a city council person."

This intimacy has also traditionally muted partisan differences. Tom Walters, a Republican state representative of the old guard, is close to a handful of Democrats in the legislature, particularly those with deep roots in the state. "Some of my good friends are Democratic legislators in the House and Senate," Walters told us, "just because they have been here long enough to have a big vision for Wyoming."

Here again, scale matters. With 93 members in its entire state legislature (62 in the House and 31 in the Senate), only Alaska's, Hawaii's, Nevada's, Nebraska's and Delaware's are smaller.[6] Cathy Connolly, a Democrat who represented a House district centered on the

---

[6] National Conference of State Legislators, "Number of Legislators and Length of Terms in Years," June 19, 2024, https://www.ncsl.org/resources/details/number-of-legislators-and-length-of-terms-in-years.

college town of Laramie for 14 years, appreciated the intimacy of the 62-member House. Despite being surrounded by Republican lawmakers, she found it easy to make friends there. She's well-liked by old guard Republicans, and that is essential for Democrats like her. "If I want to have a voice, it's with Republicans," she told us. "It's all about relationships."

One establishment Republican who has enjoyed working closely with Connolly is Sue Wilson, a Yale graduate and social studies teacher who represented northern Cheyenne for a decade, before stepping down in 2022. Wilson doesn't downplay her differences with Connolly. "She's a professor at UW, she's a lesbian. We disagree on probably 80% of life," Wilson told us. But those differences didn't prevent them from working together. "We have co-sponsored bills together [on] worker's comp" and other issues, Wilson noted. That 20 percent of life they shared was enough to form a working relationship.

Those relationships have also been easier to make because Republicans have been traditionally committed to keeping national issues out of state politics. As Nick Reynolds, a journalist and astute observer of Wyoming politics, told us: "There are some unwritten rules, like you don't bring national politics into statehouse issues." That rule is connected to the state's conservative values, a mix of parochialism, a fierce sense of independence, and distrust of federal power. As Susan Stubson noted: "We hate it when the federal government or someone not in our state tells us how to manage ourselves. That's part of the libertarian thing." But it's more than that. It's also a governing philosophy that grows up in a politics built on local, personal ties, rather than one driven by social media and cable news. And that makes it easier for the handful of Democratic legislators to seek influence in the reddest state in the union.

Not everyone, though, likes the old prohibition against keeping national issues out of state politics. The new Republican insurgents in Wyoming politics are consumed with national issues. They want bills on immigration, guns, abortion, critical race theory, and election integrity—all of which are considered national concerns by the old guard.

Such demands seem so out of keeping with Wyoming's political traditions that the old guard says out-of-state rabble rousers are to blame.

As one typical member of the old party insisted: "It's a lot of new people to the state, flooding out of California," bringing their priorities with them.

There seems to be some truth to this assertion. Wyoming has become the most transient state in the union: A majority of people born there no longer live in the state, and a majority of people who live in Wyoming were born in another state.[7] Many newcomers are conservatives, looking for a refuge from their more progressive home states.[8] And they are increasingly running for office. Leo Wolfson, who covers local politics for the *Cowboy State Daily*, has noticed the changes. "It used to be that when someone moved to a new state, it took some time to get to know the local leaders, history and general lay of the land before he or she would dive into local or state politics," Wolfson reported.[9] Not anymore. Currently, about one-third of new right legislators are not Wyoming natives.[10]

Many of the conservative newcomers consider themselves to be "political refugees" from blue or purple states, like California and Colorado. "Many have come with cautionary tales about what they believe could happen in Wyoming if left unchecked," Wolfson noted. One good example is Jeanette Ward. When she first ran for office, Ward described herself as "a political refugee from corrupt Illinois." In her former state Ward said her daughter faced a suspension for not wearing a mask in school. It was the straw, she said, that broke the camel's back.[11] As Ward's story and others like her's show, national polarization is driving the Republican civil war in Wyoming. Shaped by conflict with Democrats in blue states, these new right activists don't enter Wyoming politics to distribute liquor licenses or fix the state's tax structure. They are there to win battles they lost in blue states.

---

[7] Thảo-Nguyên Bùi et al., "A Growth Perspective on Wyoming," CID Faculty Working Paper No. 432 (Harvard University, March 2023), 3, 43.

[8] On this tendency generally, see Bill Bishop, *The Big Sort: Why the Clustering of Like-Minded America Is Tearing Us Apart* (Mariner Books, 2009).

[9] Leo Wolfson, "Move to Wyoming and Then Instantly Run for Legislature Is a Real Trend," *Cowboy State Daily*, June 6, 2024.

[10] Kerry Drake, "Departing Legislators Set Stage for Critical GOP Primary Showdowns," WyoFile, April 16, 2024, https://wyofile.com/departing-legislators-set-stage-for-critical-gop-primary-showdowns/.

[11] Brendan LaChance, "Candidate Questionnaire: Jeanette Ward for House District 57," *Oil City News*, July 1, 2022.

But while Wyoming's new right is consumed with fighting issues that matter beyond Wyoming's borders, they don't matter much to everyday life within the state. Thus, those of the new right busy themselves chasing phantoms that haunt the state, including undocumented immigrants, critical race theory in its public schools, and subterranean threats to the Second Amendment. Such crusades, which mostly serve to express identity, leave other, more serious problems neglected.

Take immigration, for example. Historically, there has been very little concern about immigration in Wyoming. That's not surprising given that there are very few undocumented immigrants who settle in the state. In both absolute and relative terms, Wyoming is not impacted much by immigration compared to other states. A Pew study estimates that there are about 5,000 undocumented immigrants in the state, which represents about 1 percent of the population.[12] What's more, they are mostly drawn to Jackson, a blue area of the state that feels like a separate republic to most natives. That leaves Wyoming's reddest counties essentially untouched by immigration.

Even so, the issue of immigration has grown in salience as Republican politics has nationalized in Wyoming. Recently, for example, the state party has considered a resolution that would formally declare English the official language of the United States. Traditional Republicans in Wyoming never thought this action was necessary given that such symbolic measures have nothing to do with governing the state. But the new insurgents see it differently. "Immigration without assimilation is an invasion," said Scott Brown, a delegate from Lovell, a town with fewer than 3,000 residents.[13]

In the statehouse, meanwhile, a group of new right legislators have been introducing a bill year after year that would ban sanctuary cities and towns. Among them is Chuck Gray, who was recently elected secretary of state and was an early candidate against Cheney before

[12] Pew Research Center, "U.S. Unauthorized Immigrant Population Estimates by State, 2016," February 5, 2019, https://www.pewresearch.org/hispanic/interactives/u-s-unauthorized-immigrants-by-state/.

[13] Leo Wolfson, "Wyoming GOP Committee Votes for 'English as Official Language' Resolution," *Cowboy State Daily*, May 6, 2022, https://cowboystatedaily.com/2022/05/06/wyoming-gop-committee-votes-for-english-as-official-language-resolution/.

Hageman entered the race. Gray and his allies know well that there are not any sanctuary cities or towns in the state of Wyoming. In fact, Gray acknowledged as much when he said of sanctuary cities: "It is important that we get ahead of this issue."[14] The bill keeps going down because the old line Republicans don't think there is anything to get ahead of. "On the ground, it's not significant," one told us. "It's only the national political environment that made it significant."

While there are undocumented immigrants here and there in Wyoming, there doesn't seem to be any critical race theory in its public schools. In fact, the subject of race is neglected altogether. In Natrona County—the second most populous county in the state behind Laramie—the word "racism" never appears in the school curriculum. And the terms "slave" and "slavery" appear only three times.[15] Even in Laramie, the only college town in the state, the school curriculum seems fairly uninterested in race. Its high school curriculum, for example, focuses squarely on traditional topics like World War II and the Great Depression. The apparent neglect of race is unsurprising given that the social studies' standards set by the state board of education make no mention of the subject.[16]

Of course, it's possible that some Wyoming teachers venture into these topics. It's also possible, even likely, that some handful of them introduce some version of the *New York Times'* 1619 Project to their students. But if that is so, no opponent of critical race theory has been able to identify such a case, even though they have a strong interest in finding one.

---

[14] Brendan Lachance, "Wyoming House Kills Bill Banning 'Sanctuary Cities and Counties' in the State," *Oil City News*, February 13, 2020, https://oilcity.news/wyoming/legislature/2020/02/13/wyoming-house-kills-bill-banning-sanctuary-cities-and-counties-in-the-state/.

[15] Morgan Hughes, "Lawmakers, State Superintendent Propose Bill to Fight Against Critical Race Theory in Schools," *Casper Star-Tribune*, September 14, 2021, https://trib.com/news/state-and-regional/lawmakers-state-superintendent-propose-bill-to-fight-against-critical-race-theory-in-schools/article_fd81b8d5-7d5e-5ad6-821e-00da0ee255cd.html.

[16] "Wyoming Social Studies Content and Performance Standards," https://edu.wyoming.gov/downloads/standards/2018/Social-Studies-Standards.pdf.

Undeterred by any evidence that radical ideas are filtering into Wyoming's public schools, the new Republican insurgents are pushing bill after bill, all aimed at stopping critical race theory from being taught. As is the case with sanctuary cities, it's an issue they want to "get ahead of." For example, Brian Schroeder, appointed superintendent of public education in 2022, called one of the bills "a necessary step stemming the tide of an insidious worldview that has become the default ideology in so many public institutions across our country, from government agencies to corporate human resource departments to teacher training programs."[17] At other times, though, Schroeder insisted that the tide had already drowned Wyoming's public schools. His two "top priorities," Schroeder explained, are putting "parents back in charge of education" and removing "indoctrination from our classrooms."[18]

Such claims have bewildered old guard Republicans. While they share a concern about the turn history education has taken elsewhere, they don't consider it a problem in Wyoming or ever likely to become one. When we asked Gail Symons, a longtime party activist, about these critical race theory bills, she couldn't understand all the attention they're getting given that "it's not being taught anywhere in the state of Wyoming." But because the new insurgents have been so shaped by the national media, Symons says, they're worried about Wyoming's schools. "They take all the talking points that show up on Fox News," Symons lamented. "And they think the folks on Fox News—most of whom have never been to Wyoming—[know] what's going on in their own state and their own community." In frustration, Symons has pressed these nationalized conservatives to provide evidence that some version of critical race theory is being taught in Wyoming's schools, only to be told: "'Well, I'm sure it is somewhere, well I'll have to get back to you.'"

Some of the crusaders against critical race theory acknowledge this problem, which is why they're pushing the Civics Transparency Act, a bill that would require school districts to post all of their teaching materials online. The bill seems to presume that parents don't have a sense

[17] Kerry Drake, "Save Timmy! Wyo GOP Seeks to 'Protect' White Kids from History," *Casper Star-Tribune*, February 22, 2022, https://wyofile.com/save-timmy-wyo-gop-seeks-to-protect-white-kids-from-history/.

[18] See candidate profile, WY Vote, https://wyvote.vote/view/candidate-profile/entry/brian-schroeder-5836/.

of their children's education, a supposition that old guard Republicans reject. This is especially so in Wyoming where communities are small and intimate. As one establishment legislator told us: "They speak of it as though it's there, and yet they know all their teachers and they know their teachers aren't teaching it."

Not only do some in the old guard regard such bills as a solution in search of a problem, like good conservatives they also worry about their unintended effects. Some, for example, say that these bills' broad prohibitions against indoctrination seem to ban the expression of any shared moral commitments. Republican state senator Jeff Wasserburger, a former teacher, was reluctant to support the bill because he thought much classroom instruction, including the teaching of the civil rights movement, does reflect a particular point of view—and justly so. For that reason, he said, "I think we're headed down the wrong path."[19] Such fears were not abated by Ogden Driskel, a Republican senator who flirts with Holocaust deniers. When the senator made his case for the new Civics Transparency Act, he argued that students should be exposed to all sides of the Holocaust. "There's a full variance on what happened and how it happened," Driskill said. "Should both sides of that be taught? To me the answer is absolutely. You need to have everything from 'it was the most atrocious thing that ever happened' to 'here's people who say it didn't happen.'"[20]

Other old guard critics of the new critical race theory bills worry that a different conservative ideal is at stake: local control. Traditionally, the state of Wyoming has set general education standards, while granting broad authority to local schools to design their own curricula in ways that suit the communities they serve. But now some old guard Republicans worry that this governing philosophy is being upended by a flurry of bills that seek to dictate education policy from Cheyenne. For example, John Brown, a party activist in the Fremont County GOP,

[19] Victoria Eavis, "Wyoming Senate Passes Critical Race Theory Ban," *Casper Star-Tribune*, February 23, 2022, https://trib.com/news/state-and-regional/govt-and-politics/wyoming-senate-passes-critical-race-theory-ban/article_cac9666c-a8ad-5ba0-b47b-328dbd1d16ff.html.

[20] Better Wyoming, "Wyo. House Education Committee Kills School Censorship Bill," March 9, 2022, https://betterwyo.org/wyo-house-education-committee-kills-school-censorship-bill/.

takes the principle of local control seriously. When these bills come up for discussion in his county party, Brown asks his fellow activists: "Why are you for the state telling the local school board what to do? If you don't like your school board, elect better school board members."[21]

Like so many other national crusades, though, probably the worst effect of the new bills targeting critical race theory is simply all the time it consumes in the legislature. These bills must be drafted, amended, and debated, diverting the legislature's attention away from real local needs and concerns. That should continue for the foreseeable future since none of these bills have been passed through both houses of the legislature, assuring there will be more like them.

While anti-racist education is not coming to Wyoming anytime soon, neither is gun control. Wyoming is the gun mecca of the United States. Compared to other states, it has the most guns per capita, and it's not close. A distant second is New Mexico, where the per capita rate of gun ownership is more than four times lower.[22] About two-thirds of all Wyoming adults live in a household where guns are present, according to a RAND survey.[23] These findings are not surprising given the popularity of hunting there: About one out of every four residents have a hunting license.[24] Wyoming also boasts one of the largest populations of veterans, on a per capita basis.[25]

All of this contributes to a strong gun culture. A study that attempted to measure gun culture across the American states found that Wyoming was only rivaled by Alaska—a state that also has an unusual number

[21] See also Jasmine Hall, "Senators Continue to Push Forward Critical Race Theory Limitations Bill," *Wyoming Tribune Eagle*, February 21, 2022, https://www.wyomingnews.com/news/in_our_schools/senators-continue-to-push-forward-critical-race-theory-limitations-bill/article_91bbc7c0-1c59-57b0-abb7-bb6a2c6f11e0.html.

[22] Cameron Porter, "Gun Ownership Mapped: How Many Guns Each State Had in 2022," *Hunting Mark*, April 18, 2023, https://huntingmark.com/gun-ownership-stats/.

[23] Terry L. Schell et al., "State-Level Estimates of Firearm Ownership," RAND, 2020, https://www.rand.org/pubs/tools/TL354.html.

[24] Meagan Drillinger, "States with the Most Registered Hunters," *Stacker*, January 25, 2023, https://stacker.com/your-state/states-most-registered-hunters.

[25] World Population Review, "Veterans by State, 2023," https://worldpopulationreview.com/state-rankings/veterans-by-state.

of veterans and licensed hunters.[26] Wyoming's gun culture—like that found in other western states such as Montana, Colorado, and Idaho—has more distant origins, one rooted in the violence of frontier societies. In such places, a strong gun culture developed early because, as one historian put it, the "arm of justice was often far away."[27]

Thus, the regulation of guns has been weak in Wyoming from the beginning. As a history of gun laws in the state found, peaceable "open firearm carriage has almost always been allowed everywhere." The state's strong devotion to gun rights continues into the present day. In fact, the state now allows citizens to carry concealed weapons without a permit as well.[28] When *Guns and Ammo* magazine assessed the extent to which each state regulates guns, it found that Wyoming had the fewest restrictions, concluding: "Wyoming is a true paradise for gun owners with a strong showing across the board."[29]

Nor does that paradise seem endangered. As Wyoming House member Landon Brown, a fierce defender of Cheney and the establishment, told us: "It is under absolutely zero duress." "Nobody is taking your damn guns in the state of Wyoming." Another told us: "You will be hard pressed to find someone in the state who is legitimately anti-gun."

The broad, bipartisan appeal of guns in Wyoming was highlighted in a humorous election campaign video posted by Sara Burlingame, a former progressive Democratic state legislator and current executive director of the LGBQT-rights group Wyoming Equality. Addressing the claim that activists like her were trying to "take away your guns," Burlingame retorted, "No thanks! I got my own!" as she aimed and shot.[30]

---

[26] Claire Boine et al., "What Is Gun Culture? Cultural Variations and Trends Across the United States," *Humanities and Social Sciences Communications* 7, no. 21 (2020): 1–12.

[27] George A. Mocsary and Debora A. Person, "A Brief History of Public Carry in Wyoming," *Wyoming Law Review* 21, no. 2 (2021): 341–68, https://scholarship.law.uwyo.edu/cgi/viewcontent.cgi?article=1450&context=wlr.

[28] Mocsary and Person, "Brief History of Public Carry," 343, 366.

[29] Keith Woods, "The Best States for Gun Owners: Ranked for 2022," *Guns and Ammo*, August 18, 2022, https://www.gunsandammo.com/editorial/best-states-for-gun-owners-2022/463592.

[30] Sara Burlingame, "Sara Burlingame 4 Wyoming House 44," Facebook, October 2, 2018, https://www.facebook.com/voteburlingame/videos/267745340536559/.

Nor was this unusual. Democrat Stan Blake, who served from 2007 to 2021 as the state representative from Green River, boasted an "A" rating from the National Rifle Association. Blake laughingly described to us an exchange he had while attending a political conference with other state-level Democratic officials when "somebody from California just started talking about gun control. And a fellow [from Wyoming] next to me, says [to the Californian] 'What are you talking about?! I got a rifle in the back of my truck half the day when I'm driving. I might have to euthanize a cow that broke his leg. I might have to shoot a wolf.'"

Even looking to Wyoming's neighbors in the Mountain West—states that have seen more migrants from California—it's hard to see any real threat to Second Amendment freedoms. The exception might be Colorado, which has become a purple state in recent years. But even there, wide gun rights prevail. Colorado only managed to pass the most modest of restrictions: a law called "The Vote Without Fear Act," which bans citizens from openly carrying a gun near polling stations during elections.[31]

But these facts don't matter for those who define the party wholly around a handful of national concerns. For them there is no politics below the culture wars that divide red and blue America. And so, year after year, they convulse Wyoming's legislature in debates over guns. The pace of these bills has also increased as failed bills from previous sessions get reintroduced in new ones. By 2021, the state's Senate Judiciary Committee heard its fourth gun bill in only its second session. A total of eight gun bills were introduced that year.[32]

State senator Anthony Bouchard—who perhaps more than any Wyoming politician has mimicked Trump—has been at the center of this surge. He sponsored at least three different gun bills in recent years.[33] One attempted to repeal a handful of exemptions to

[31] Emma Tucker, "These Are the Gun Control Laws Passed in 2022," CNN, December 31, 2022, https://www.cnn.com/2022/07/30/us/gun-control-laws-2022/index.html.

[32] Nick Reynolds, "Gun Bills Playing Outsized Role in Already Gun-Friendly Wyo Politics," WyoFile, March 26, 2021, https://wyofile.com/gun-bills-playing-outsized-role-in-already-gun-friendly-wyo-politics/.

[33] For recent bills, see State of Wyoming 68th Legislature, "Senate District 06: Senator Anthony Bouchard," https://www.wyoleg.gov/Legislators/2022/S/2030.

Wyoming's essentially unregulated gun culture. Recall that it's generally legal in the state to carry a concealed weapon without a permit or license. But not absolutely anywhere. The state allows gun bans on government and school grounds. For Senator Bouchard and his allies, this is an intolerable violation of their constitutional rights. And, so, they have been sponsoring bills that eliminate these exemptions.[34]

That effort was given new life when some delegates to the GOP state convention in 2018, held at the University of Wyoming, were cited for carrying weapons on school grounds. Even after they were cited and warned by university police, several delegates continued to bring weapons to the convention. From their perspective, the university police have no grounds to sanction them since they regard any restriction on the right to bear arms as unconstitutional. This is why Senator Bouchard called the citations "a crime."[35]

It was a crime for another reason though: Banning guns at a GOP state convention interferes with the expressive ends of the new identity politics. Once politics becomes fundamentally about the expression of identity, laws that get in the way are oppressive. In effect, the university police made the new conservatism a crime.

No recent gun bill, though, generated more controversy than the Second Amendment Preservation Act. The bill, passed in 2022, prohibits state officials from enforcing federal gun laws that are unconstitutional. Those who do are subject to a year in prison and a $2,000 fine.[36] The establishment managed to kill a much more punitive version of the bill,

[34] See, for example, Brendan Lachance, "Wyoming Again Seeing Effort to Repeal Gun Free Zones, Allow Conceal Carry at Colleges and UW," *Oil City News*, February 8, 2021, https://oilcity.news/wyoming/legislature/2021/02/08/wyoming-again-seeing-effort-to-repeal-gun-free-zones-allow-conceal-carry-at-colleges-and-uw-2/.

[35] Joel Funk, "University of Wyoming Police Explain Handling of Open Carry Defiance at GOP Convention," *Casper Star-Tribune*, August 25, 2018, https://trib.com/news/state-and-regional/university-of-wyoming-police-explain-handling-of-open-carry-defiance-at-gop-convention/article_11d51445-befc-515c-acc6-526600753a5b.html.

[36] Jasmine Hall, "Gordon Signs Second Amendment Protection Bill," *The Sheridan Press*, March 22, 2022, https://www.thesheridanpress.com/news/regional-news/gordon-signs-second-amendment-protection-bill/article_8db63066-aa05-11ec-a9c4-6741c4bc4777.html.

one that would have subjected public officials to lawsuits.[37] That was unacceptable to the hard-line members of the new right, many of whom voted against the weaker version.[38] And while many members of the establishment voted for the watered-down bill and were happy to put the whole contentious issue to rest, they also thought the whole exercise was a charade. "That bill was a joke," Landon Brown told us; it "was all for show."

Perhaps the best evidence of the nationalization of Wyoming politics has been the panic over the integrity of its elections. For those who worry that Democrats stole the election, Wyoming's voting system seems like a particularly odd source of anxiety. In 2020 Trump won Wyoming with approximately 70 percent of the vote, a larger share of the vote than any state in the union.[39] Trump also performed marginally better that year in Wyoming than any other Republican presidential candidate in the past 20 years (see Table 4.1).

Table 4.1 Share of Vote for Republican Presidential Candidate, Wyoming

2000	67.8%
2004	68.9%
2008	64.8%
2012	68.6%
2016	68.2%
2020	69.9%

Source: https://www.270towin.com/states/Wyoming.

37 Kerry Drake, "Wyoming's Gun Advocates Are Forming a Circular Firing Squad," WyoFile, April 19, 2022, https://wyofile.com/wyomings-gun-advocates-are-forming-a-circular-firing-squad/.

38 Brendan Lachance, "Governor Signs Second Amendment Protection Act, Restricting Wyoming Officials from Enforcing 'Unconstitutional' Federal Firearms Regulations," *Oil City News*, March 22, 2022, https://oilcity.news/legislature-community/2022/03/22/governor-signs-second-amendment-protection-act-restricting-wyoming-officials-from-enforcing-unconstitutional-federal-firearms-regulations/.

39 See election results data from CNN, "Presidential Results," https://www.cnn.com/election/2020/results/president.

Nonetheless, a panic gripped much of the Wyoming GOP in the wake of the 2020 election. State officials and legislators were flooded with demands to investigate the reliability of Wyoming's election system. Even before the election, the state party was pushing for election integrity. One recent resolution urged "Wyoming lawmakers to develop election audit systems and manual recounts to further ensure the integrity of our election systems."[40] County parties followed suit. In Park County, for example, the GOP insisted that Wyoming's voting machines were unreliable. Its chair, Larry French, put it plainly: "We don't trust the machines."[41] And so, at the party's county convention in 2022, its first resolution focused on election integrity, insisting that election integrity is of "paramount importance."[42] Thus, French and his allies argued that all of Park County's ballots should be hand-counted. When that request was denied, the party said that county officials—including the sheriff and county commissioner—should step down from office for violating both the Wyoming and US Constitutions.[43]

The movement for election integrity took hold in Wyoming, in part, because the party is increasingly defined by activists and politicians with national platforms. They include Mike Lindell, who held an online symposium for activists in the wake of the 2020 election. At the symposium, Lindell cast doubt on the reliability of voting machines and hence the election results everywhere, not just in the battleground states Trump lost. Following Lindell's event, Wyoming officials noticed a surge in citizen concerns about the state's election system. As one official in the office of the secretary of state noted: "We have gotten a lot of emails

---

[40] "Resolutions Passed by the Wyoming Republican Party Central Committee Since State Convention May 2018," https://www.wyoming.gop/_files/ugd/d8b5a1_b2dcca034b6948b3aacec5ee11222349.pdf.

[41] Maggie Mullens, "Election Distrust Persists, Solutions Mired in Politics," WyoFile, April 14, 2022, https://wyofile.com/election-distrust-persists-solutions-mired-in-politics/.

[42] Park County Republican Party, "Final Resolutions," March 12, 2022, https://www.parkcountyrepublicans.org/_files/ugd/65f35a_67fd2538a0434097b5f5b40d961a738b.pdf.

[43] Soleil Teal, "Park County Wyoming Officials Violate Their Oaths in GROSS Negligent Fashion," *Wyoming News*, October 26, 2022, https://wyomingnews.tv/news/local/park-county-wyoming-officials-violate-their-oaths-in-gross-negligent-fashion/.

and a lot of calls with concerns about the integrity of our elections" since Lindell's symposium.[44]

In 2022, Dinesh D'Souza's film *2000 Mules* made a splash in Republican circles across the country. The movie claimed to lay bare a Democratic conspiracy to commit massive voter fraud through the use of ballot boxes in battleground states. We noticed it was playing at the downtown theater in Casper during the summer of 2022. At the time then-candidate Chuck Gray held numerous private showings all over Wyoming as part of his successful campaign for secretary of state.

Everyone seemed abuzz about the movie. At a restaurant in Sheridan, when a local swung by our table to briefly catch up with the activist we were interviewing, she asked: "Did you see *2000 Mules?* It's a movie about how the 2020 election was compromised. They used geo-tracking and security cameras. Proof right there." Even the film's producer was a familiar figure: When we rented our car, the manager—an immigrant named Ricky D'Souza—said people in Wyoming often ask him if he is related to Dinesh D'Souza. (He's not.)

To assuage fears the legislature passed a voter identification law and made it a penalty to disclose election results before polls close.[45] Meanwhile, the then-secretary of state, Ed Buchanan, developed a road show to debunk lingering doubts after the integrity of Wyoming's elections. He traveled around the state, presenting evidence to county parties that the state's elections are secure.

His case was strong. The state's voting machines could not be hacked since they were not even connected to the internet. Buchanan invested all this work to restore faith in Wyoming's elections because he understood the stakes: "If folks ever lose faith in our elections, then all is lost because they will lose faith in their government, they will lose faith in law enforcement, they will lose faith in the legislature, in my office [and] anyone that's in a position of authority."[46]

---

[44] Nick Reynolds, "Officials Face Growing Pressure to Audit Wyo Elections," WyoFile, August 25, 2021, https://wyofile.com/officials-face-growing-pressure-to-audit-wyo-elections/.

[45] Mullens, "Election Distrust Persists."

[46] Dustin Bleizeffer, "Voter ID Bill Advances in Legislature," WyoFile, February 25, 2021, https://wyofile.com/voter-id-bill-advances-in-legislature/.

Buchanan's efforts did little, though, to put the anxieties of activists to rest. "He's taking a ton of flak," one member of the establishment told us. Exhausted by the flak, Buchanan accepted a district judgeship in 2022, a post he had long coveted. Looking for an interim replacement, Governor Mark Gordon then had to select a candidate nominated by the party's central committee. With only candidates from the new MAGA-verse to choose from, he selected Karl Allred, a foreperson at a gas plant and one of the violators of the University of Wyoming's gun ban.[47] The larger rebuke to Buchanan and the old guard, though, happened a few months later, when Chuck Gray was elected Wyoming's secretary of state. Gray made election integrity his central issue, calling for audits and stricter election laws.[48]

To those who have observed Wyoming politics for years, Gray's ascension was bewildering. Cathy Connolly, who serves in Wyoming's House as the minority leader, noted: "In the past, taking up a national crusade would have gotten nowhere. But [election integrity] has gotten traction [even though] it makes no sense. And there is no solution to a non-problem."

Wyoming does have real problems though. The biggest, according to the Republican establishment, is the state's tax structure. With no personal income tax and low sales taxes, the state must rely heavily on taxes on its mineral sector to fund its services. A majority of state revenue comes from oil, gas, and coal. The figure varies considerably, though, because the mineral sector has long been driven by boom-and-bust cycles.[49]

It is also in decline. Coal production, in particular, is collapsing. Nationwide, coal production hit a 50-year low in 2020.[50] Those

---

[47] Maya Shimizu Harris, "Gov. Gordon Appoints Karl Allred as Interim Secretary of State," *Casper Star-Tribune*, September 29, 2022, https://trib.com/news/state-and-regional/govt-and-politics/gov-gordon-appoints-karl-allred-as-interim-secretary-of-state/article_2a4fa128-4042-11ed-8064-9f8694ca8db7.html.

[48] Nick Reynolds, "Election Audit Bill Fails," WyoFile, August 5, 2021, https://wyofile.com/election-audit-bill-fails/.

[49] Andrew Graham, "How Does Wyoming's Tax Structure Compare to Other States," WyoFile, May 16, 2017, https://wyofile.com/wyomings-tax-structure-compare-states/.

[50] Hugh Cook, "Even Though Wyoming Coal Production Has Increased, Experts Say the Industry Is Set to Decline," Wyoming Public Radio, January 14, 2022,

changes have hit Wyoming hard. The state collects half a billion dollars less from coal taxes than it once did, cratering its budget. One journalist called the decline a slow-moving "catastrophe." As he explained: "Wyoming pays for state government—everything from public schools and road maintenance to public health and the criminal justice system—primarily with revenue collected from the oil, gas and coal industries. Of those three, coal has been both the stable bedrock—not prone to the up-and-down swings of the oil and gas markets—and at times the largest contributor."[51] And now it's going away.

Wyoming's Republican establishment is determined to do something about it. When we asked Representative Tom Walters to name Wyoming's biggest challenge, his response came quickly: "The biggest thing is our tax structure. We have a structure that is too heavily reliant on our mineral sector." He estimates that about 75 percent of the state budget is mineral-related—once investment income off mineral revenues and property taxes on the mineral sector are included. Thus far the state has survived by pulling from reserves, but that can't continue for much longer. Because that is only a stopgap measure, though, Walters says he votes for tax increases to stabilize the state's revenue streams.

Given the seriousness of this problem, the old guard is particularly irked by the endless parade of non-issues that come before the legislature. An exasperated JoAnn True told us that critical race theory became a "huge thing" for the party: "This was a top five issue for the state party, not revenue for the state or the need to replace oil and gas, or K–12 education funding being cut. Not these things that are impacting 99 percent of the population." Representative Landon Brown agrees with both Walters and True. "We're creating bills to fix issues that don't truly exist," he told us. "We have spent more time discussing non-issues, than fixing our state budget issue."

---

https://www.wyomingpublicmedia.org/natural-resources-energy/2022-01-14/even-though-wyoming-coal-production-has-increased-experts-say-the-industry-is-set-to-decline.

[51] Andrew Graham, "Bedrock Erosion: How Much Has Wyo Lost to Coal's Decline?," WyoFile, June 4, 2019, https://wyofile.com/bedrock-erosion-how-much-has-wyo-lost-to-coals-decline/.

The problem is already catching up to ordinary Wyomingites. In 2022 the legislature discovered that the state faces an enormous budget shortfall—approximately $193 million—for education in 2023 and 2024.[52] Those amounts are expected to balloon even higher by 2025, perhaps to as much as $880 million. "The hand-writing is on the wall," said Mark Gordon, the state's establishment governor. "The can we kick down the road every year, it is broken. We have to deal with this issue."[53]

While that can keeps getting kicked down the road, Chuck Gray was thinking of an 11-mile stretch of road that bypasses Dick Cheney's hometown of Casper. Gray decided to sponsor a bill that renames it the "President Donald J. Trump Highway."[54] It didn't get by the old guard in Wyoming's House, who refused to take it seriously. But Gray's bill was indicative of broader changes in the Wyoming GOP. In the past, it would be difficult to imagine any legislator sponsoring a bill to rename a Wyoming highway after a politician who had never even bothered to campaign in the state.

* * * * *

Not long ago, the national GOP centered the concerns of local parties. While the GOP nationalized congressional races in 1994 by running on a "Contract with America," this so-called Republican revolution also tried to roll back federal power. In fact, many of these "revolutionaries" thought of themselves as latter-day Anti-Federalists, determined to recapture state and local sovereignty from an overweening federal government. They delivered on some of those promises. One of their early legislative achievements was the passage of the Unfunded Mandates

52 Maya Shimizu Harris, "Wyoming Faces $193 Million School Funding Shortfall," *Casper Star-Tribune*, April 29, 2022, https://trib.com/news/local/education/wyoming-faces-193-million-school-funding-shortfall/article_ef45fc53-9735-5bef-b36c-323acf391e61.html.

53 Brendan Lachance, "Gordon: K–12 Education 'the Biggest Elephant' as Wyoming Works to Avoid $885M Budget Deficit," *Oil City News*, March 2, 2021, https://oilcity.news/wyoming/legislature/2021/03/02/gordon-wyoming-k-12-education-the-biggest-elephant-as-legislature-works-to-avoid-885m-budget-deficit/.

54 See State of Wyoming 68th Legislature, "HB0153: President Donald J. Trump Honorary Highway-Designation," https://www.wyoleg.gov/Legislation/2022/HB0153.

Reform Act, a law that curbed the imposition of onerous and expensive regulations on states and localities. A couple of years later, the Republican Congress passed a bipartisan welfare reform bill, which, despite serious shortcomings, also shifted some control over social provision back to the states.[55]

Whatever else might be said of the Contract with America, it also included a series of concrete policies, including some that touched American pocket books. During the 1996 budget negotiations, for example, Republicans successfully pushed for a $500 tax credit for families.[56] Thus, they took everyday governance with at least some seriousness.

By the time the next wave of conservative populism crashed in 2010, much had changed. Cable and online news emerged as important agents of political socialization, both of which emphasized national issues and personalities.[57] The Tea Party was shaped by those influences. Unlike the Republican revolutionaries of 1994, the Tea Partiers elected in 2010 showed much less interest in devolving power back to the states. And they showed little inclination toward governing more generally. Political scientist Rachel Blum found that Tea Partiers were much less interested than other Republican members in discussing a wide range of domestic issues. They included unemployment and the regulatory burden on small businesses—problems that should be of interest to a party that seeks to represent middle America. For that reason some early enthusiasts of the Tea Party soon became disenchanted, particularly libertarians looking to shrink the size of the federal government. As a leader in the Libertarian Party explained: "The Tea Party was too wrapped up in symbolism to be serious about addressing the problems of the nation."[58]

[55] Linda Killian, *The Freshman: What Happened to the Republican Revolution* (Basic Books, 1999), 6, 27, 346–50, 416.

[56] Killian, *Freshman*, 304.

[57] Hopkins, *Increasingly United States*, 126–29.

[58] Rachel B. Blum, *How the Tea Party Captured the GOP* (University of Chicago Press, 2020), 64, 94–97, 104.

By the time Liz Cheney first ran for the Wyoming House in 2016, the Republican Party had already been remade by the new nationalized conservatism. Arguably, her success in the 2016 race owed something to those changes. She won the race despite weak ties to the state. Unlike so many other politicians who ascended to state-level offices, Cheney had not come up through Wyoming politics She had never served in the state legislature or as a mayor. She didn't go to college in the state, opting for Colorado College and then the University of Chicago. And Cheney spent most of her childhood years in the Washington suburbs. What she mostly had was a nationally prominent name, one that local Wyomingites took great pride in. She also enjoyed a wide national network of donors: Some 75 percent of the money she raised came from out of state.[59]

Meanwhile, one of her main rivals was Tim Stubson, who had deep roots in the state and its politics. Stubson grew up in Casper, earned a law degree at the University of Wyoming, and had served in the Wyoming House for 9 years. He emphasized these ties when he ran against Cheney. In an early interview he gave for the *Wyoming Tribune Eagle*, Stubson said he was running because, "it's very important to have someone in that seat that has a history of working on those [local] issues in the state, that knows the people of the state." And when he was asked directly about his qualifications, Stubson first stressed his local roots, reminding the reporters of his "lifetime" of service to Wyoming.[60] Stubson's appeals were not enough. He—and another candidate with deep roots in the state—lost handily.

By 2022, the race for Wyoming's House seat became even more nationalized. Harriet Hageman did sometimes note her local roots, but unlike Stubson she never placed them at the center of her campaign. Instead, Hageman stressed her close ties to Trump. Meanwhile, donations from out of state dwarfed in-state contributions for both candidates,

---

59 Paul Kane, "Liz Cheney Launches a New Brand in Wyoming," *Washington Post*, August 16, 2016, at https://www.washingtonpost.com/politics/another-cheney-rises-in-a-republican-party-led-by-trump/2016/08/15/a2f817a0-6267-11e6-8b27-bb8ba39497a2_story.html.

60 "Tim Stubson—U.S. House, Republican," YouTube, 40 min., 35 sec., https://www.youtube.com/watch?v=l81nalYHS6s.

especially for Cheney. By the fourth quarter in 2021, a mere 1.3 percent of her $2-million haul came from Wyomingites.[61]

These changes scrambled old alliances. By 2022 Cheney had been embraced by many in the once skeptical old guard, including Stubson. No longer regarded as just a symptom of the nationalization of Wyoming politics, Cheney was fighting to vanquish its worst expressions. And now that she has been exiled from Wyoming politics forever, the question remains: Can Stubson and his ilk mount a successful counterrevolution against the new national conservatism?

In the next chapter we'll see how the establishment is striking back, working to broaden its party and save it from the age of identity politics. That means that governing conservatism might have a future, and not just a past, worthy of greater appreciation.

---

[61] Mike Koshmrl, "Hageman Outpaces Cheney in Early in-state Contributions," WyoFile, February 2, 2022, https://wyofile.com/hageman-outpaces-cheney-in-early-in-state-contributions/.

5

The Establishment Strikes Back

LIZ CHENEY'S 2022 PRIMARY RACE was never as close as her supporters in Wyoming imagined. On election day roughly two out of every three Wyomingites swung for Hageman. Hageman even carried Natrona County, the center of which is Dick's hometown of Casper. Only in Albany and Teton—Wyoming's two bluest and most educated counties—did Cheney prevail.[1]

Cheney's fate mirrored that of the other House candidates who defied Trump by voting for impeachment after January 6th. Of the other nine members, four retired, and three were primaried by Trump-aligned candidates. Only two survived.[2] And, as this book goes to press, Trump is set to reoccupy the White House in 2025. These outcomes are a testament to Trump's unique and lasting popularity among Republican primary voters.

Trump's enduring power is partly due to the weakness of Republicans in the US Senate. They had an opportunity to rid

---

[1] They are the only two counties in which a majority of the adult population had college degrees.

[2] Amber Phillips, "What Happened to the 10 House Republicans Who Voted to Impeach Trump?," *Washington Post*, August 17, 2022, https://www. washingtonpost.com/politics/2022/03/01/what-happened-10-house-republicans-who-voted-impeach-trump/.

their party of Trump by voting to convict him in his second impeachment trial. But, once again, they let their party and nation down, all in the hope that Trump's cultish power would fade on its own.

Yet, it's also the case that Trump's power has been far from absolute. Many candidates who tried to ape him—like Kari Lake in Arizona, Doug Mastriano in Pennsylvania, and Herschel Walker in Georgia—lost their statewide races in 2022. Others, like Lauren Boebert, seemed unbeatable. Yet, she barely managed to hang on to power, winning by just 564 votes. And all this in a midterm election that was supposed to be good for Republicans. Those outcomes seem to be due, in part, to a sizable block of more traditional Republicans who voted for Democratic candidates. The defectors ranged from 13 percent of Republican voters in Arizona to 18 percent in Pennsylvania.[3]

What's more surprising is what has been happening in Wyoming. Even in the Trumpiest state in the union, the Republican establishment is far from dead. That's been hard to see because Cheney's defeat has been interpreted as a last stand, rather than just a battle lost in a war yet to be won.

If one looks at politics on the ground, Wyoming's establishment is more entrenched than Cheney's defeat might suggest. Yes, its enemies have a lot of momentum. Each election year, new right Republicans chip away just a bit at the establishment's control of the state legislature. They control the state party's central committee and most county organizations as well. But it's also the case that the old guard is beginning to take these threats more seriously. In varied ways the establishment is counter-mobilizing against the new right, efforts that have met with success. After the new right members of the House formed a political action committee (PAC), the Wyoming Freedom PAC, in 2023, for example, the establishment responded by creating the Wyoming Caucus.[4]

---

[3] Hannah Fingerhut, "Anti-Trump GOP Voters Mostly Loyal in 2022, but not Entirely," Associated Press, March 12, 2023, https://apnews.com/article/trump-republicans-maga-loyal-2022-election-750a18b724adod999e9d9d793cobcf7d.

[4] Leo Wolfson, "An Election Off Year, Millions Raised and Spent on Wyoming Politics in 2023," *Cowboy State Daily*, January 4, 2024.

A close look at the 2022 Republican primaries and the 2023 election for party representatives also suggests that the establishment isn't folding up its tent. Many so-called Republicans in name only (RINOs) in the state legislature survived primary challenges in 2022, including one who was a vocal critic of Trump. Meanwhile, some of the Trumpiest incumbents lost. Thanks to these successes the old guard still controlled the legislature after the 2022 election. In 2023, meanwhile, the establishment actually reclaimed party organizations in Fremont, Johnston, Lincoln, and Uinta Counties.

Similar civil wars are playing out in parties and legislatures in red states all across the nation, most of which are just below the national media's radar. The fate of the GOP will be decided by a thousand such skirmishes, not a handful of high-profile races like Cheney's.

These internecine struggles have a parallel on the left. In progressive institutions from universities to cities like San Francisco, elites within the liberal establishment—or "normies" as they're sometimes called—are counter-mobilizing too, pushing against the new identity politics. Establishments, conservative and progressive, also confront a challenging asymmetry in their war against identitarians. Their foes have much momentum, partly because they are more energized than those who tend to align with comparatively tempered establishments. As political scientists Steve Teles and Rob Saldin remind us, it's radicals who often win these internecine partisan battles because they are more committed to doing the work of democracy. Moderates, they say, often "lose out to the 'wingnuts' because those on the ideological extremes, to their credit, actually do the difficult, long-term labor that democratic politics rewards: showing up, organizing, and devoting themselves to building durable institutions for political and intellectual combat."[5]

But that doesn't mean "normies" can't do that work, too. As this chapter will show, they are fighting back in Wyoming, even taking back some of the party organizations they had lost. So long as that is true, the long-term outcome of the Republican civil war is hard to see.

* * * * *

    [5] Steven M. Teles and Robert P. Saldin, "The Future Is Faction," *National Affairs* (Fall 2020), https://www.nationalaffairs.com/publications/detail/the-future-is-faction.

It's difficult to know precisely how many new versus old right representatives make up the Wyoming legislature. This is partly because, until recently, formal party caucuses have not existed. And although a Wyoming House Freedom Caucus formed in 2020, it doesn't publish the names of all of its members—and there still isn't a similar organization in the Wyoming Senate. As a further complication, not every Republican legislator necessarily feels closely aligned with either camp, though the vast majority do.

A good, if imperfect, way to categorize all members is to use legislative scorecards developed by Honor Wyoming. As we mentioned in Chapter 3, Honor Wyoming is a new right group that tries to shame RINOs. As such, it uses members' voting records to distinguish members of the Republican establishment from "true" Wyoming conservatives. The site classifies Republicans into three categories: "high integrity" (true conservatives), "questionable integrity" (ambiguous conservatives), and "low integrity" (fake conservatives), with most aligning at the poles.

By this metric, the establishment still enjoyed a majority by 13 seats in the House and 6 seats in the Senate after the 2022 elections. However, those margins are narrowing and imperiled at times by a handful of Republicans with uncertain loyalties. And some estimates place the margins a bit closer. Wyoming's House Freedom Caucus, for example, recently claimed that it needed to pick up about 10 additional seats in 2024 to effectively control the chamber.[6]

With 21 open seats in the legislature, 2022 could have been the year the old establishment fell. But that is not what happened despite remarkable turnover. Some 27 new Republicans were elected to the Wyoming House of Representatives, a massive infusion of legislators for a body with 62 members. Based on our analysis of Honor Wyoming's data in June 2024, 12 are aligned with the old guard, 11 are clearly identified with the new right, while 4 seem non-aligned. Of the 11 new right candidates, 5 won open seats, 5 defeated Republican incumbents, and 1 beat a Democratic incumbent. Two of the Republican incumbents were defeated by very narrow margins: one race was decided by

---

[6] Leo Wolfson, "'We Need 10 More': Freedom Caucus Pushes for More Members at Town Hall, Looks Ahead to 2024," *Cowboy State Daily*, April 15, 2023.

12 votes, another by 56 votes. Only one incumbent from the old guard lost decisively: Not surprisingly, it was Pat Sweeney, a genuine RINO.

In the Senate, only four new members were elected in 2022, an unsurprising outcome given its staggered terms and smallness of the body (31 seats overall). The four new senators run the gamut, a microcosm of the Wyoming GOP. They include Eric Barlow, a dedicated old guard Republican and former House speaker; Stacy Jones, a newcomer who defeated new right conservative Tom James; Bob Ide, a fervent Trumpist who was at the capitol on January 6th; and Evie Brennan, a former intensive care nurse with ties to the new right. Looking at the results as a whole in both chambers, they suggest that each faction is roughly equally matched and well entrenched in the legislature.

While there are no strong patterns, looking more closely at individual races shows that establishment candidates can win in what might seem like unfavorable circumstances. One of the more remarkable successes for the establishment was the survival of Landon Brown, a representative from Cheyenne. From the beginning, Brown had been a staunch defender of Liz Cheney. They were kindred spirits. Like her, he was shaken by the events on January 6th. That day he called his parents in tears. "There is no way that I'll vote for him again," he affirmed over his hot cup of coffee at a Cheyenne Starbucks. "I will not vote for a man who I've seen hurt our country."

Brown's open opposition to Trump set him at odds with most Republicans in the state. He received a steady stream of angry calls and emails, one from a man who promised to rip Brown's face off and then feed it to his dogs. Such calls unsettled the Brown family. Landon and his wife lost sleep. Up at night, Brown wondered whether he should really run again.[7]

He would have been forgiven for simply finishing out his term, especially since his prospects of re-election didn't seem very bright. Even if he hadn't come out against Trump, Brown's voting record was also a problem. Like others in the Republican establishment, Brown had

---

[7] Victoria Eavis, "Despite Threats, Lawmaker Will Run," *Rawlins Times*, April 6, 2022, https://www.wyomingnews.com/rawlinstimes/news/despite-threats-lawmaker-will-run/article_ab976893-d2b4-5c0b-90e5-ae87220c659f.html.

run afoul of the new right Republicans for some heretical views despite a strong conservative record. He especially rankled his critics for supporting Medicaid expansion and opposing the prohibition of sanctuary cities. For these votes he was dubbed "RINO of the month" in April 2021 by WyoRINO. "When reviewing Rep. Landon Brown's (R-Laramie) voting record," the site announced, "one wonders how anyone could have such audacity to vote so much in favor of Democrat policies and yet run on the Republican ticket."[8]

Undaunted, Brown decided to run for re-election in 2022. "There is work to still be done," he said. "I feel like I have opportunities to make a difference in the state of Wyoming, and I do care about the state."[9] Like so many in the establishment, Brown also didn't downplay his opposition to Trump. In fact, he went on CNN, where he accused Trump of hijacking the GOP and said that he was unfit to be president.[10] But he made up for these remarks with a good ground game. At home in his district, Brown went door to door, hitting all of them except for those with "Trump 2024" flags. His hard work paid off. A majority of voters re-elected Brown in the 2022 primary, albeit by a narrow margin.

One advantage Brown had over Cheney is that he had much deeper roots in this district.[11] Cheney was never beloved in Wyoming because she didn't grow up there and she didn't work her way up from smaller offices to larger ones, unlike the state's governor and US senators. She also wasn't educated at the University of Wyoming; instead, she attended Colorado College for her undergraduate degree and then the University of Chicago for law school. Any one of these markers would be a liability. We were reminded of this truth when we chatted with a new right activist who complained that the state's governor, Mark Gordon, wasn't educated in Wyoming; instead, he attended "some fancy

---

[8] "RINO of the Month April 2021," https://wyorino.com/rino-of-the-month-april-2021/.

[9] Eavis, "Despite Threats, Lawmaker Will Run."

[10] Natalie Colarossi, "Trump Has 'Hijacked' GOP, Is 'Unfit for Office,' Says Republican Lawmaker," *Newsweek*, February 12, 2022, https://www.newsweek.com/trump-has-hijacked-gop-unfit-office-says-republican-lawmaker-1678714.

[11] It also helped Brown's success that his district was located in Cheyenne, where college-educated, establishment Republicans are concentrated.

school [Middlebury] back east." But at least Gordon had other things going for him, like being raised on a ranch in rural Johnson County.

Cheney's biography, though, presented her with many formidable obstacles to a political career in Wyoming politics. They were hard to overcome. In 2014, during her first bid for office in Wyoming, she tried to unseat the sitting Republican senator Mike Enzi before exiting the race when her prospects looked dim, partly because she was seen as an outsider. One poll at the time found that just 31 percent of locals considered her a Wyomingite.[12] Enzi, meanwhile, was loved and enjoyed deep roots in the state. He spent his life in Wyoming, working his way up the political ladder: first serving on Gillette's city council, then as mayor of Gillette, then the Wyoming House, then the Wyoming state Senate, and, finally, in the US Senate. And even as a US senator, Enzi remained locally oriented. As the *New York Times* noted after Cheney dropped out of the race, Senator Enzi "is well-known for his ice cream socials and for his habit of taking copious notes at town hall meetings, letting every attendee speak his or her mind before he takes the podium."[13] After that Cheney spent more time in the state, earning enough trust to win an open House seat a couple of years later. But even then her success owed much to her family name, leaving her with no deep well of trust and affection that she had built up over time.

Hence, Cheney's loss doesn't mean old-fashioned Republicans can't win in the state—or that they must pretend to be populists to do so. Consider the example of Wendy Schuler, an old guard Republican who held on to her rural district, defeating a new right primary challenger.[14] What is perhaps most impressive about Schuler's victory is that she campaigned in a nakedly anti-populist way. Schuler made no campaign pledges, beyond a general promise to represent her constituents well. "That's the only campaign promise that I made," she told us. This one promise grants her significant freedom to decide what is truly in the best interest of her constituents. It's a trust she's earned thanks to her decades as a devoted teacher and sports coach in the county. And in

---

[12] James Arkin, "Report: Cheney Fishing License Snag," *Politico*, August 6, 2013, https://www.politico.com/story/2013/08/liz-cheney-fishing-license-095230.

[13] Jonathan Martin, "For Cheney, Realities of a Race Outweighed Family Edge," *New York Times*, January 6, 2014, https://www.nytimes.com/2014/01/07/us/politics/liz-cheney-to-quit-wyoming-senate-race.html.

[14] The largest town in Schuler's district is Evanston, with about 12,000 residents.

Schuler's mind, her constituents include everyone in her sparsely populated district, not just the conservative identitarians. When Schuler tangles with them, she reminds them: "You guys think this way, but there's a whole lot of people that think differently."

While Brown and Schuler were incumbents with deep roots in their districts, some old guard Republican challengers also either won open seats or defeated new right legislators. Jon Conrad, an old guard member, defeated the notorious Karl Allred. As mentioned in Chapter 2, Allred used to intimidate his colleagues by bringing his gun into the legislature. And Lane Allred, an establishment candidate with a postgraduate degree (no relation to Karl), beat a professional cage fighter. More impressively, Stacy Jones defeated state senator Tom James in 2022. Senator James—who was also profiled in Chapter 2—seemed to be the future of the new Republican Party in Wyoming. He came from a genuinely disadvantaged background, even campaigning for his Senate seat as he delivered pizzas. Elected in 2018, James gained a reputation for incivility once in office. As one veteran Wyoming reporter observed: "James showed more disrespect for his colleagues than anyone I've ever seen at the Capitol. He frequently interrupted meetings by yelling at people."[15] And James hewed closely to the narrow, creedal agenda established by the new GOP. He even sponsored legislation that would have imposed fines and even jail time on state workers who implemented federal vaccine mandates.[16]

When Stacy Jones launched her primary campaign, she explicitly challenged the new politics. Announcing her bid for office, Jones said: "I know that in order to accomplish goals for our county and state, we need to work well with others. This is not a fight, but a collaboration to achieve results for Sweetwater County."[17] By emphasizing "collaboration" and "results," Jones gently repudiated a conservative

---

[15] Kerry Drake, "What Will It Take to Restore Legislative Decorum in Wyoming?," WyoFile, December 13, 2022, https://wyofile.com/what-will-it-take-to-restore-legislative-decorum-in-wyoming/.

[16] Mychael Schnell, "Wyoming Lawmakers to Hold Special Session on Bills to Counter Vaccine Mandates," The Hill, October 18, 2021, https://thehill.com/homenews/state-watch/577263-wyoming-lawmakers-to-hold-special-session-on-bills-to-counter-vaccine/.

[17] See campaign website for Stacey Jones, https://jones4wyoming.com/stacy-jones-announces-run-for-state-senate-district-13/.

identity politics that rests on incivility and performance. Apparently, that message resonated with the citizens of Sweetwater County. Tom James received just a third of the primary vote.

Thanks to successful old guard candidates like Brown, Schuler, Conrad, and Jones, the establishment still controlled the Wyoming legislature, at least as of 2022. The old guard, in alliance with five Democratic representatives, still ran the show. And it maintained control of critical leadership positions in both the Senate and House. Al Sommers won the powerful House speakership over new right legislator Mark Jennings, a critical victory. He has used that power to keep the new politics at bay. When the Senate—which is now closely divided between the new and old Republicans—passed a "don't say gay bill" modeled on Florida's legislation, Sommers simply didn't assign it to a House committee, effectively killing the bill.[18]

The one surprise was the election of Chip Neiman as the new House majority floor leader in 2022. Neiman, who won the position by a single vote, has been an outspoken leader of the new guard. Unlike some of his fiercer colleagues, though, Neiman has also struck conciliatory notes—and long been regarded more positively by the establishment crowd.[19] After he ascended to his new post, Neiman told reporters: "I don't believe you can come in there and say, 'It's my way or the highway.'" "I will be open to working with both views to try to find some ground where we can work together and get some good things passed," Neiman added.[20] Thus far he has shown an inclination to reach across the divide.

Still, Neiman's election was a shock to the old guard and a reminder that they are close to losing control of the House. Hence, the establishment decided to counter-mobilize more aggressively. In 2023 it formed a PAC named the Wyoming Caucus, a title that emphasizes the

---

[18] Jeff Victor, "Wyoming's 'Don't Say Gay' Bill Dies in the House," Wyoming Public Radio, February 27, 2023, https://www.wyomingpublicmedia.org/news/2023-02-27/wyomings-dont-say-gay-bill-dies-in-the-house.

[19] One, for example, told us that Neiman is more reasonable than other new right legislators.

[20] Mike Koshmrl, "Far-Right Lawmakers Prepare to Wield Their Growing Power," WyoFile, December 9, 2022, https://wyofile.com/far-right-lawmakers-prepare-to-wield-their-growing-power/.

establishment's commitment to state issues and suspicion of the new nationalized agenda pushed by the new conservatives. The leaders of the establishment are also not waiting until the next election to defend what they call the "Wyoming way" against the new nationalized identity politics. They are raising money for candidates and on the offensive. After the legislative session in 2023, Speaker Al Sommers and other House leaders wrote a sharp editorial, rebuking the new insurgents. "This session," they wrote, "we faced multiple attempts by outside Washington, D.C., interests to infiltrate the people's house like never before, encroaching on Wyoming people's priorities and promoting a narrative that is far from the truth. This effort is putting our conservative, common-sense Wyoming way in jeopardy."[21] Like Stacy Jones' campaign for the state legislature, the "Wyoming way" is a defense of a local, indigenous form of politics against a coarsening national political culture.

As this rebuke should suggest, the establishment is now less inclined to allow norm-breaking to slide. And, so, when the newly elected Harriet Hageman publicly scolded Al Sommers and his allies for killing the "don't say gay" bill, the old guard defended the Wyoming way. Leading the charge was Wyoming's elder statesman and former US senator, Al Simpson. Through the local press, Simpson called Hageman's intervention "embarrassing" and "an egregious overstep." "We never sent any mail to the Speaker of the House or the President of the Senate and if we did, they'd laugh at it."[22] Traditionally, Wyoming's small US congressional delegation has stayed out of local political squabbles.

Part of what the establishment is fighting for in its quibble with Hageman, though, isn't just the autonomy of the legislature. It's a style of politics that uses relationships rather than social media to resolve conflicts. Hageman could have simply called Sommers to express her

---

[21] Albert Sommers et al., "House Leadership: Wyoming Legislative Work Reflects Wyoming Values," *Cowboy State Daily*, March 18, 2023, https://cowboystatedaily.com/2023/03/18/house-leadership-wyoming-legislative-work-reflects-wyoming-values/.

[22] Leo Wolfson, "Hageman's Comments to State Legislative Members 'Unheard of' in History of Body," *Cowboy State Daily*, March 2, 2023, https://cowboystatedaily.com/2023/03/02/al-simpson-hagemans-comments-to-legislative-members-embarrassing-and-unheard-of/.

point of view, an option not lost on Sommers. "I think that would have been the first step, [she could have] just [given] me a ring to talk to me," he said. Instead, Hageman went straight to Twitter to rebuke the House speaker.[23]

New guard members of the state legislature are easier to sanction than Hageman. Fed up, the establishment just stripped state senator Anthony Bouchard of his committee assignments for a pattern of intimidating, intemperate speech. More than any other politician, Bouchard models himself most closely on Trump. He's promoted many of Trump's conspiracies—including claims of election fraud—and even seems to have acquired a collection of red ties, which he wears regularly. More than anything, though, it seems to be Bouchard's incivility that troubles the establishment most. Senate vice president Larry Hicks explained his support for the sanction against Bouchard, noting to local media: "When you go out on social media and impugn every member of the Legislature by calling them a swamp, slimeball, liars, that is not conduct becoming of a Wyoming state senator."[24]

Despite the rise of social media, personal ties are still powerful in a state like Wyoming. The Wyoming way endures. When Joe McGinley, chair of the Natrona County GOP, was unsuccessfully challenged by some members of the new guard, he didn't gloat or attempt to punish his enemies. Instead, he invited them out for coffee. Some accepted, and more coffee dates soon followed. Those meetings didn't put their disagreement to rest, but they did clear the air and built some good will and trust. "Those individuals despised me when I first started," McGinley recalled. "But just sitting down and having a conversation, helped with a lot of that. I think they were being misled by a small group of individuals that were manipulating them, and taking advantage of just blind trust."

McGinley's overtures are an illustration of what political theorist Aurelian Craiutu has called moderation, a many-faced and essential virtue in open societies. A moderate citizen, Craiutu says, "radiates openness and generosity toward others and refuses to practice

---

[23] Wolfson, "Hageman's Comments to State Legislative Members."

[24] Mike Koshmrl, "Wyoming Senate Takes a Stand on Civility," WyoFile, March 14, 2022, https://wyofile.com/wyoming-senate-takes-a-stand-on-civility/.

political vendettas." This generous openness springs from "the assumption that social, political, economic, moral, and cultural pluralism is an inescapable part of our modern society."[25] McGinley's moderation doesn't soften everyone, of course. Some of his foes won't even have a conversation.

Even if it were otherwise, taking back the state party requires counter-mobilization, not coffee talks. McGinley noticed that one reason the new guard had seized so many county party organizations is because many precinct elections are uncontested. Marti Halverson— a Trump stalwart and leader of the new guard—was first elected as a Lincoln County precinct committeewoman in 2000 because she simply wrote her own name in. That's all it took since there was no opposition. Halverson was elected by a single vote—her own.[26] Many of these posts go unfilled, making local party organizations easy to capture by highly motivated factions.

Natrona itself almost flipped to the other side. "We were close," McGinley recalled. "It was like fifty–fifty when I first got involved." It was close, though, because many precinct posts were unfilled. So, McGinley got more people involved, making sure that Republicans ran for every precinct post. Today, he estimates that roughly 80 percent of the county party is made up of traditional Republicans. "Engagement is key. Apathy is what leads to this," he told us. That engagement, in turn, has improved the decorum of party meetings and made involvement in the county party more appealing to traditional Republicans.

JoAnn True, an old guard conservative from Natrona, has appreciated these changes. Prior to McGinley's intervention, True recalled, party meetings "started getting really nasty." She even left the party for a spell. But True was pulled back in by McGinley, who told her that the party was becoming "crazy" because reasonable Republicans like herself were disengaged. Today True is the vice chair of the county party and, along with allies like McGinley, firmly in charge of the county party.

---

[25] Aurelian Craiutu, *Faces of Moderation: The Art of Balance in an Age of Extremes* (University of Pennsylvania Press, 2017), 21, 23.

[26] Mike Koshmrl, "Halverson, 'Grandma' of Wyo's Shift Right, Has a Zeal for Helping Others," WyoFile, May 9, 2023, https://wyofile.com/halverson-grandma-of-wyos-shift-right-has-a-zeal-for-helping-others/.

In more rural Fremont County, traditional party activist John Brown has observed the power of well-organized minorities close up. Disgusted by the county party's censure of senator Cale Case, Brown noted that "it's the vocal minority who show up to the central committee meetings, and they generally get their way." "It's a little disheartening." As in other county parties, many precinct positions also simply go unfilled.

The result is a very small number of party activists who run the show. There are 84 precinct positions in Fremont County, yet only 18 total votes were cast when Case was censured and only 11 in favor of it. Thus, out of 84 potential votes, 11 voted for Case's censure. "That's how it gets hijacked," JoAnn True noted. "They say they're the grassroots because they are the county party, but really that is a fiction they tell themselves."

In the 2023 party elections, the establishment party struck back, making the fiction harder for the insurgents to believe. The establishment regained control of the party in four counties: Lincoln, Fremont, Johnson, and Uinta. These upheavals unseated some of the most prominent MAGA-aligned party activists from leadership positions. In Lincoln County the whole leadership team turned over. Wade Hirschi seized the chair from Marti Halverson, an activist who calls herself "one of the grandmothers" of the new conservatism.[27] The same wholesale turnover happened in Uinta County. There, traditional Republicans defeated the entire executive committee, including the infamous Karl Allred. He gained notoriety for taking a gun into senate committee meetings.[28] And in Fremont—the same county party that voted to censure its state senator Cale Case just months earlier—the traditional candidate Scott Harnsberger won the chair.[29]

The outcome has already made a tangible difference in Fremont County. In 2023 the new guard tried to censure US Senator Cynthia

---

[27] Koshmrl, "Halverson, 'Grandma' of Wyo's Shift Right."

[28] Greg Johnson, "'Traditional' Republicans Take Back Uinta County GOP in Party Coup," *Cowboy State Daily*, March 15, 2023, https://cowboystatedaily.com/2023/03/15/traditional-republicans-take-back-uinta-county-gop-in-party-coup/.

[29] Leo Wolfson, "Halverson Ousted as Wyoming County GOP Elections Move Toward 'Traditional Republican' Leadership," *Cowboy State Daily*, March 20, 2023, https://cowboystatedaily.com/2023/03/20/halverson-ousted-as-wyoming-county-gop-elections-move-toward-traditional-republican-leadership/.

Lummis for voting in favor of the Respect for Marriage Act, a law that affirmed the federal government's support for same-sex marriage. Senator Lummis defended her vote not by arguing for the dignity of same-sex love as a California senator might but by recognizing the need for social tolerance in a pluralistic nation. She commented after her vote: "For the sake of our nation today and its survival, we do well by taking this step, not embracing or validating each other's devoutly held views, but by the simple act of tolerating them." Her defense did not buy her much cover with members of Fremont County's new guard. They proposed a censure resolution that said the Respect for Marriage Act was an "existential threat to the God-given family structure" and at odds with both the party's platform and its grassroots constituents.

But it was at odds with many of the newly elected precinct committeemen and -women, who voted down the censure resolution. When the new guard proposed a sternly worded letter instead, it was voted down as well.[30] These failed resolutions marked a major shift in a local party that just 1 year prior had censured their local senator for supporting Medicaid expansion.

Everywhere, the newly elected establishment leaders stressed their commitment to restoring the Wyoming way. Ron Micheli, the new state committeeman in Uinta, said he is part of a "movement in the party to bring people together and be more inclusive." "I do believe that people in the state are tired of the lack of civility and the bullying politics," he added.[31] Hirschi—the new leader in Lincoln County—struck the same notes. "I definitely would like to see a greater unity in the party," he said. "We have to remember we don't necessarily all have the exact

[30] Maya Shimizu Harris, "Fremont County GOP Attempt to Censure Lummis Fails," *Casper Star-Tribune*, January 16, 2023, https://trib.com/news/state-regional/fremont-county-gop-attempt-to-censure-lummis-fails/article_ea68a180-95b5-11ed-90d9-ffa7aa87385d.html; Clair McFarland, "Fremont County GOP Unsuccessful in Censuring Lummis over Same-Sex Marriage Vote," *Cowboy State Daily*, January 17, 2023, https://cowboystatedaily.com/2023/01/17/fremont-county-gop-unsuccessful-in-censuring-lummis-over-same-sex-marriage-vote/.

[31] Maya Shimizu Harris, "Far-Right Leaders Ousted in County GOP Elections," *Casper Star-Tribune*, March 21, 2023, https://trib.com/news/state-and-regional/govt-and-politics/far-right-leaders-ousted-in-county-gop-elections/article_61d073d0-c804-11ed-988f-c770acc1f8c5.html.

same idea on how to implement those principles and the platform, but let's sit down and work together and come together."[32]

The traditionalists didn't win everywhere. They fell just short in Campbell County, which fell back into the hands of the new guard. And the state central committee is still controlled by the new right, despite some significant gains by establishment candidates. The new guard activists see the battle clearly. Biffy Jackson, chair of the Uinta County GOP, even dismissed the relevance of the Cheney–Hageman standoff that so riveted Wyoming in the summer of 2022; instead, she insisted, "precinct races are the most important."

Yet, even Frank Eathorne, the party's state chair, felt at least some tremors from the counterrevolution: 2023 marked the first year Eathorne faced a serious challenger, having faced only token opposition in 2019 and running unopposed in 2021.[33]

The race pitted two Franks from opposite sides of the tracks against one another. Frank Moore, Eathorne's challenger, is a poster child of the old elite traditionalists. Moore is the owner of a frozen lamb company who served in the Wyoming House as well as on the board of directors for the Kansas City Federal Reserve Bank.[34] Eathorne, meanwhile, worked in pest control and as a parole officer. He is also associated with a militia and was on the Capitol grounds on January 6th.

Their campaign messages reflected the growing fault lines within the party. Like other establishment candidates, Moore emphasized his big-tented, conciliatory approach to leadership. "I think the Republican Party needs to be brought together, and I think what it's going to take is some listening and just some understanding," he said.[35] Eathorne,

[32] Duke Dance, "Hirschi Elected Chairman of Lincoln County GOP," *SVI News*, March 22, 2023, https://svinews.com/hirschi-elected-chairman-of-lincoln-county-gop/.

[33] Leo Wolfson, "Frank Eathorne Wins Third Term as Wyoming Republican Party Chairman in Landslide," *Cowboy State Daily*, May 6, 2023, https://cowboystatedaily.com/2023/05/06/frank-eathorne-reelected-as-wyoming-republican-party-chairman/.

[34] Leo Wolfson, "Douglas Sheep Rancher Frank Moore to Run Against Frank Eathorne to Lead State Republican Party," *Cowboy State Daily*, April 19, 2023, https://cowboystatedaily.com/2023/04/19/douglas-sheep-rancher-frank-moore-to-run-against-frank-eathorne-to-lead-state-republican-party/.

[35] Maya Shimizu Harris, "Former Converse County Lawmaker Will Challenge Eathorne for Top Wyoming GOP Post," *Casper Star-Tribune*, April 19, 2023,

on the other hand, stressed the need for the party to stick to its creedal agenda as well as its deeper redemptive purpose. "The platform is our standard," he said. "We need to continue to govern red, and we're gonna save this state and save this nation." Eathorne won the race by a 2-to-1 margin and is comfortably in charge, at least for now.[36] But the tide is starting to turn inside the state party. Eventually, it may sweep more establishment figures back into power.

At the same time, the establishment is pushing for institutional reforms that would lead to greater power within the state party. Currently, the state party central committee is composed of three members from each county, which favors more rural, populist areas. The reform effort, led by Senator Cale Case, would instead base representation on the central committee on the number of registered Republicans in each county.[37] The bill failed partly because many members don't think the state has the authority to regulate political parties. But Case's salvo is another sign that the establishment is now mobilized and on the offensive.

The establishment's relentless war to prevent the MAGA-fication of the Republican Party—including its devotion to governance and democratic norms—also left us with the sense that many of its critics are missing something. In the next chapter, we call for a fuller, more nuanced account of the much maligned Republican establishment

https://trib.com/news/state-and-regional/govt-and-politics/former-converse-county-lawmaker-will-challenge-eathorne-for-top-wyoming-gop-post/article_a1277062-deaf-11ed-ab6d-7be993d2fae2.html.

36 Maya Shimizu Harris, "Eathorne Wins Third Term as Leader of Wyoming Republican Party," *Casper Star-Tribune*, May 6, 2023, https://trib.com/news/state-and-regional/govt-and-politics/eathorne-wins-third-term-as-leader-of-wyoming-republican-party/article_efe7b23a-e9f8-11ed-9995-ebee5eabfa93.html.

37 Leo Wolfson, "Cale Case Says Larger Counties Should Have More State-Level Party Influence," *Cowboy State Daily*, December 20, 2023.

6

The Republican Establishment and Its Critics

NOT MANY CONCERNS UNITE AMERICAN intellectuals these days. One that might come close is the belief that the Republican establishment has been an abject failure. Liberals and Never-Trumpers say it too easily capitulated to Donald Trump and has thus imperiled liberal democracy. Progressives say the GOP establishment is too dominated by rapacious plutocrats. And MAGA-aligned intellectuals say old guard Republicans can't be counted on to fight the woke left. For all their differences, all three of these critiques suggest that Republican elites suffer from a deficit of character. They are, it seems, simply too spineless and self-regarding to rule well. To varying degrees, our findings should call these arguments—and the deeper assumptions on which they rest—into question.

In recent years, some of the most trenchant critics of the Republican establishment have come from the defenders of liberal democracy, including conservatives who broke sharply from Trump. These liberal voices have rightly highlighted the GOP's troubling pattern of acquiescence in the face of the ex-president's norm-breaking.[1] As we

---

[1] Steven Levitsky and Daniel Ziblatt, *How Democracies Die* (Broadway Books, 2018).

have shown, however, the picture in Wyoming is more complicated. Yes, there are few vocal Republican critics of Trump in Wyoming. There should be many more Landon Browns. But it's also the case that Wyoming's old guard constitutes a resistance nonetheless. After all, Wyoming's establishment has been busy debunking right-wing conspiracies, defending deliberative political norms, and stressing the importance of governance. A fuller account of the Republican establishment should include not just nationally prominent elites but also the many state and local politicians who fight every day to stop the MAGA-fication of their party.

A longer-standing criticism of the Republican establishment comes from progressives who say it mainly is a self-serving plutocracy, working against the interests of its working-class voters. For decades, in fact, they have hoped that the white working class would topple the affluent oil magnates, doctors, and bankers who direct the Republican Party's policy agenda. As the previous chapters have shown, that may ultimately come to pass, and not just in Wyoming. The once high and mighty are being brought low.

But if that revolution from below ultimately succeeds, progressives might awkwardly find themselves rooting for the counterrevolution from above. At least in Wyoming, some progressives are already making this reassessment. One is Anne MacKinnon, the former editor-in-chief at the *Casper Star-Tribune*. She and her progressive friends disliked the old guard when it was firmly in command but now wish they could all be returned to power. "A lot of my friends," she told us, "thought those guys in the 80s were just terrible. And now they seem like total heroes compared to those jerks that we've gotten in the legislature now."

The old party was never as terrible as the left supposed because its longings for a class war rested on a distortion. They assumed that the Republican elite was greedily preoccupied with lining its bulging pockets at the expense of its working-class voters. Critics believed these Republican elites did so largely by mobilizing cultural grievances to acquire power but then sought the narrow interests of the ultrarich once in office. Thomas Frank even explicitly likened the GOP establishment to the oil oligarchs of Arab states, calling it a "manipulative ruling class that had for decades exploited an impoverished people."[2] Political scientists Jacob Hacker and Paul Pierson come to roughly the same conclusion. In their view, the Republican establishment cynically used populist rhetoric to maintain its power so that it could pursue the interests of the wealthy. "As the GOP embraced plutocratic priorities," they observe, "it embraced a set of electoral strategies that were increasingly strident, alarmist, and racially charged."[3]

Such criticisms were so influential that even some conservative intellectuals have embraced them. After Republicans did worse than expected in the 2022 midterms, Sohrab Ahmari blamed it on a greedy GOP business class: "Republican economic policy remains overwhelmingly beholden to a donor class of plutocrats and high corporate managers." "These faux populists," Ahmari continued, "remain indifferent to issues like wages and workplace power, health care and the depredations of speculative finance."[4] In his new book *Tyranny Inc.*, Sohrab Ahmari has doubled down on this thesis, so much so that he is now praised by intellectuals on the social democratic left.[5]

These progressive critiques, we argue, fail to see a political tradition of noblesse oblige and public spiritedness that tempered the GOP establishment's pursuit of its economic self-interest. It furthermore has been blind to the way the establishment's very elitism allowed it to play a critical role in modeling a democratic cultural style among Republicans.

For most MAGA-aligned intellectuals that is precisely the problem with the Republican establishment. In their view, the party needs to summon the rugged toughness of the American working class to fight an existential battle against "woke" liberals. The professional class is inadequate because it is too devoted to norms of civility, compromise, and even respect for the rule of law itself. Thus, while country-club

---

[2] Thomas Frank, *What's the Matter with Kansas? How Conservatives Won the Heart of America* (Metropolitan Books, 2004), 239–40.

[3] Jacob S. Hacker and Paul Pierson, *Let Them Eat Tweets: How the Right Rules in an Age of Extreme Inequality* (Liveright Publishing, 2020), 4.

[4] Sohrab Ahmari, "Why the Red Wave Didn't Materialize," *New York Times*, November 10, 2022, https://www.nytimes.com/2022/11/10/opinion/republicans-midterms-workers-populists.html.

[5] Sohrab Ahmari, *Tyranny, Inc.: How Private Power Crushed American Liberty—And What to Do About It* (Forum Books, 2023).

Republicans are fit to rule in normal times, they cannot win the current war. Here again, partisan polarization is driving the Republican civil war.

The critique of the GOP establishment from MAGA sympathizers fails to notice that the new right insurgents they champion have much in common with what they consider to be the nation's foremost existential threat: the "woke" left. As we've shown, both the new Republican insurgents and the social justice left are obsessed with identity, which inclines them to police ideas and expression. New right legislators are also not the least bit interested in governance even in a conservative mecca like Wyoming, where there is no left to constrain their power.

* * * * *

A hero of Never-Trumpers and liberals, Liz Cheney is rightly celebrated for her defense of our constitutional democracy. Unlike most of her Republican colleagues, she waged an unrelenting war against Trump, culminating in her leadership on the January 6th Committee. Much like their Republican legislators in the Congress, few in Wyoming's GOP establishment are willing to confront Trump's demagoguery directly.

These similarities can mislead us, though. Yes, the Wyoming establishment hasn't vocally called out Trump's misbehavior very often, but neither has it sat on its hands. As the previous chapter showed, it has defended the norms and democratic traditions that Trump and his ilk have degraded. In 2022, the Natrona County GOP even called on Frank Eathorne—perhaps Wyoming's most Trump-like figure—to resign his chair of the party, calling him unfit for the office.[6]

This resistance has been easy to miss because books on the right focus on national politics, neglecting a much larger universe of Republican politicians and activists, most of whom have been ignored by historians and political scientists. In the world of these more provincial Republicans, the likes of Sean Hannity and Tucker Carlson are remote, distant figures.

---

[6] Sara Sammons, "Natrona Republican Party Resolution Calls for Immediate Resignation of State GOP Chairman," *Oil City News*, June 20, 2022, https://oilcity.news/community/wyoming-community-2/2022/06/20/natrona-republican-party-resolution-calls-for-immediate-resignation-of-state-gop-chairman/.

Because most books on the Republican Party focus on the national GOP, they have also highlighted its near total acquiescence to Trump. In *How Democracies Die* Steven Levitsky and Daniel Ziblatt lament that "most Republican leaders closed ranks behind Trump" in 2016, which "normalized the election." Thus, Levitsky and Ziblatt say Republican leaders lost an opportunity to shift enough votes away from Trump to defeat him. And after the election, few national leaders openly criticized Trump's incivility and dishonesty. It's as if they simply sat on their hands, waiting for the Trumpist storm to blow over. Levitsky and Ziblatt conclude by calling for a reformed GOP, one that addresses the "bread and butter concerns" of ordinary Americans and marginalizes the extremists in its ranks.[7]

As troubling as such accounts are, it isn't the whole story. Here and there, a fuller picture of the establishment's resistance beyond the Beltway has bubbled up from below. The January 6th Committee shined a rare but bright light on this larger world as a stream of state and local Republican officials made their case against Trump's election lies. In addition to Republican-appointed judges, these were the conservative officials who saved our democracy from a far deeper constitutional crisis. This book picks up where that commission left off by shining an even brighter light on a state-level GOP establishment.

It's less clear why members of state-level Republican establishments seem tougher than their national counterparts. Maybe they simply felt that they had less to lose than members of Congress. Or maybe—as the Wyoming story suggests—the power of these Republicans also rests more firmly on local, personal ties. Thus, they are more insulated from the pressures of the 24-hour national news media and Trump's ever vigilant monitoring. Trump made an example of Liz Cheney but neglected Wyoming's Landon Brown. Brown simply didn't attract enough national media attention to incite Trump's ire. The insulation and personalism of local politics is sometimes a frustration for those new insurgents who hope to capture the attention of journalists and patrons outside their small orbit.[8]

---

7 Levitsky and Ziblatt, *How Democracies Die*, 69–71.

8 See, for example, the case of New Jersey's Ed Durr. Matt Friedman, "New Jersey's MAGA Cinderella Faces a New Test: Getting Reelected when Both Parties Want

This resistance to the new identity politics has a counterpart on the left—and it, too, is also sometimes missed by critics of "wokeism." In progressive institutions—city governments, newsrooms, and universities—establishment elites are reasserting the importance of liberal virtues, especially viewpoint diversity and civility. You can see it in the opinion pages of *The New York Times*, which seemed as if they might become captured by left-wing orthodoxy in the wake of George Floyd's murder. But instead it hired columnist John McWhorter, a strong critic of modern-day anti-racism, as well as conservative David French, formerly at the *National Review*. Prior to the overturning of *Roe v. Wade*, the *Times* also featured guest essays by pro-life writers.[9]

Universities and colleges, including Middlebury, Johns Hopkins, the University of Texas, Duke, and Arizona State University, have instituted new programs and schools to advance these liberal values as well.[10] Our own Claremont McKenna College created the "Open Academy," an initiative that advances freedom of expression, viewpoint diversity, and constructive dialogue.

These programs seem remarkably similar to one in the otherwise distant world of Wyoming Republican politics. When we discovered the Frontier Republicans—a party organization in Wyoming that promotes the Open Academy's values—we felt a sense of common purpose and challenges.[11] Other evidence suggests that the academy in general has become somewhat less dominated by progressives' priorities. For example, after about 2020—a year sometimes referred to as "peak woke"—scholarship on bias and discrimination slackened a bit, shifting

---

Him Gone," *Politico*, March 12, 2023, https://www.politico.com/news/2023/03/12/ed-durr-new-jersey-maga-00086052.

[9] See, for example, Tish Harrison Warren, "Why the Feminist Movement Needs Pro-Life People," *New York Times*, November 28, 2021; Erika Bachiochi, "I Couldn't Vote for Trump, but I'm Grateful for His Supreme Court Picks," *New York Times*, December 7, 2021.

[10] The programs include the Davis Collaborative in Conflict Transformation at Middlebury, the Agora Institute at Johns Hopkins University, the Civitas Institute at the University of Texas, the Democracy and Higher Education Program at Duke, and the School of Civic and Economic Thought and Leadership at Arizona State University.

[11] Frontier Republicans, "Who We Are," https://www.frontierrepublicans.com/who-we-are.

to other topics.[12] On college campuses, liberal normies can feel the "vibe shift" as well.

Thus, across the political spectrum and in a wide institutional landscape, there are new efforts underway to combat the excesses of identity politics. These are underway among progressive intellectuals as well. Consider, for example, Eitan Hersh's popular book *Politics Is for Power*. Its main thesis is that politics is not about self-expression in the service of constructing a political identity or remaining ideologically pure— it's about building coalitions so that we can collectively address hard problems. And if you think otherwise, Hersh says, you're doing politics wrong. In fact, you're not really doing politics at all.[13] The old guard leaders of the Wyoming Republican Party could not agree more.

Ordinary Democratic voters are pushing back too. Eric Adams, an ex-cop, won the New York City mayoral race in 2021, largely by stressing a pragmatic approach to fighting crime.[14] Even in America's left-coast cities, governing Democrats have been elevated into office. After the San Francisco school board busied itself renaming a third of its schools instead of managing COVID well, they were recalled. Even in an age consumed with identity, results matter to many ordinary voters. As one disgruntled parent said: "It's the people rising up in revolt in San Francisco and saying it's unacceptable to abandon your responsibility to educate our children."[15] The citizens of Seattle even went a step further: They elected a Republican city attorney. Promising to

---

[12] Musa al-Gharbi, "Wokeism Is Winding Down," *Compact*, February 8, 2023, https://compactmag.com/article/woke-ism-is-winding-down; Musa al-Gharbi, "The 'Great Awokening' of Scholarship May Be Ending," *Heterodox Academy*, February 26, 2023, https://heterodoxacademy.org/blog/the-great-awokening-of-scholarship-may-be-ending/.

[13] Eitan Hersh, *Politics Is for Power: How to Move Beyond Political Hobbyism, Take Action, and Make Real Change* (Scribner, 2020). See also Yascha Mounk, *The Identity Trap: A Story of Ideas and Power in Our Time* (Penguin, 2023).

[14] Katie Glueck, "Eric Adams Is Elected Mayor of New York," *New York Times*, November 2, 2021, https://www.nytimes.com/2021/11/02/nyregion/eric-adams-mayor.html.

[15] Thomas Fuller, "In Landslide, San Francisco Forces Out 3 Board of Education Members," *New York Times*, February 16, 2022, https://www.nytimes.com/2022/02/16/us/san-francisco-school-board-recall.html.

address rising crime in the city, she beat out a police abolitionist who had celebrated the destruction of property.[16]

All these various forms of counter-mobilization against identity politics have expressed core liberal commitments. Among them is an acceptance of pluralism and the consequent need to manage our diversity by considering and balancing interests. The assertion of these commitments in so many institutional and ideological settings is a reminder of the power and vitality of America's liberal tradition.

*****

While Liz Cheney is celebrated as a hero of liberal democracy, her father, Dick, has long been a symbol of the supposedly craven Republican establishment. His insider contacts from years in government allowed him to make millions from the oil company Halliburton once he re-entered private life—and when he returned to public service as vice president, Cheney continued to work nice deals for his former employer. As *The Atlantic*'s Conor Friedersdorf concluded: "There is no better example of the problematic 'revolving-door' relationship between government and private enterprise than Dick Cheney and Halliburton."[17]

The Cheneys—both Liz and Dick—also purchased homes near Jackson in Teton County, a place so wealthy one scholar described it as a "billionaire wilderness."[18] That's hyperbole, of course. Still, the county is the wealthiest in the United States, a winter playground for the rich and famous, including Harrison Ford, Sandra Bullock, and plenty of Wall Street tycoons. The place is so insular that residents of Wyoming towns like Sheridan and Casper don't think it's really even part of the cowboy state. And it's hard to blame them. For example, at a

---

[16] Andrew Jeong, "Seattle Elects Republican as City Attorney, Rejecting Police Abolitionist Who Celebrated Property Destruction," *Washington Post*, November 6, 2021, https://www.washingtonpost.com/nation/2021/11/06/seattle-election-prosecutor-ann-davison/.

[17] Conor Friedersdorf, "Remembering Why Americans Loathe Dick Cheney," *Atlantic*, August 30, 2011, https://www.theatlantic.com/politics/archive/2011/08/remembering-why-americans-loathe-dick-cheney/244306/.

[18] Justin Farrell, *Billionaire Wilderness: The Ultra-Wealthy and the Remaking of the American West* (Princeton University Press, 2021).

Teton County environmentalist event publicizing the importance of preserving grasslands, half the attendees already knew a lot about the subject from having been on African safaris; only one person there, however, could locate Thermopolis, just a few hours' drive away. A quip we heard repeatedly was, "Jackson is just a short drive from Wyoming."

As the example of the Cheney clan suggests, critiques of the old establishment contain some truth. The old guard was too insular and practiced self-dealing on occasion, and Wyoming's Republican establishment was no exception. As Nick Reynolds, one of Wyoming's best political journalists, acknowledged, the establishment was "a good-old boys club." Much of their work is still done in the shadows. "They stay in the house of the appropriations committee chairman," Nick noted, "and they hash out the budget behind the scenes." It has long been a world in which a few wealthy men iron out their differences over cocktails.

Those conversations over cocktails invite self-dealing. There has been a tendency, for example, for the old guard to intervene in local land-use decisions when they think their interests are at stake. In one case, Bob Nicholas, chair of Wyoming's appropriation committee in the House, sponsored a bill that helped out Phil Nicholas—a prominent lawyer who represents the University of Wyoming and, as it happens, is Bob's brother. The bill, which was signed into law, allowed the university to dig wells that the city of Laramie insisted were part of its water supply. For its part, the city noticed the conflict of interest. "I think there is a larger issue that goes beyond just the city of Laramie's water complaints," the city's mayor observed. "And that's the willingness of the legislature to do the bidding of their friends and interest groups on the outside."[19] In another recent case, Eli Bobout—who served in both Wyoming's Senate and House—co-sponsored a bill that would have given his own oil and gas company a tax break. Such conflicts of interest, some journalists alleged, are common in the Wyoming legislature, though they go unpoliced.[20]

---

[19] Nick Reynolds, "Legislature Referees Water Squabble, Raising Local Control Issue," WyoFile, April 26, 2021, https://wyofile.com/legislature-referees-water-squabble-raising-local-control-issue/.

[20] Kerry Drake, "When Is Conflict of Interest a Conflict? Almost Never," WyoFile, March 13, 2018, https://wyofile.com/conflict-interest-conflict-almost-never/.

More systematic research suggests that such cozy relationships are hardly unusual in America's state legislatures. One recent study, for example, found that state legislators are especially responsive to the economic policy preferences of its wealthiest interests. This is true of both parties. As the authors of this study conclude: "We have ample evidence that the wealthy, more often than not, do call the shots."[21] What's more, Wyoming is not an especially corrupt state by American standards. It's certainly nothing like the infamous Louisiana or Illinois. In fact, Wyoming seems to have average levels of public corruption compared to other American states, perhaps even less.[22]

Like highly educated progressives, some members of the establishment are also prone to looking upon their rivals in the white working class as ignorant rubes. When we asked one lawyer and Republican activist from a rural county if he noticed any differences between the pro- and anti-Trump Republicans in his county, he confessed: "Well, now you're going to see my prejudice come out. It seems to me the more thinking people [oppose Trump]. I hate to say this, but maybe you've got to think a little deeper about your candidate." Others said that the new insurgents don't respect the old norms because they're not "adults" or "gentlemen." One called the new insurgents' behavior "sophomoric"—a term, she doubted, they would even "know the meaning of." Or, as another noted, they "brought the trailer parks into politics," while yet another said they do "things you might see in a bar." Such characterizations echo Hillary Clinton's infamous use of the term "deplorables" to describe Trump's supporters.[23]

For some establishment Republicans, the awareness of being part of an elite is softer. Sue Wilson, a Republican who has served in the Wyoming House since 2013, is sometimes appalled by the conservative causes of the new right, such as its campaign to make English the official language. "I don't know from what talk show they get these thoughts,"

---

[21] Gerald C. Wright and Elizabeth Rigby, "Income Inequality and State Parties: Who Gets Represented?," *State Politics and Policy Quarterly* 20, no. 4 (2020): 395–414.

[22] Harry Enten, "Ranking the States from Most to Least Corrupt," *FiveThirtyEight*, January 23, 2015, https://fivethirtyeight.com/features/ranking-the-states-from-most-to-least-corrupt/.

[23] Such prejudices run deep in the broader culture, of course. See Nancy Isenberg, *White Trash: The 400-Year Untold History of Class in America* (Penguin, 2017).

she mused. Wilson is certainly a social conservative. But she's also a Yale graduate who has lived in different parts of the United States, traveled internationally, and taught Spanish much of her life. These experiences have introduced more cosmopolitan sensibilities into her conservative worldview.

Class prejudices are evident outside of Wyoming as well. When Marjorie Taylor Greene wrote "Pelosi's gazpacho police" rather than "gestapo police" she was mocked for the mixup. Less noted was how unfamiliar gazpacho is to Americans outside the managerial professional elite. The Spanish soup is a favorite of the professors who lunch at Le Pain Quotidien in our college town but hard to find in dining establishments in red-state America. Thus, to many Americans it may have seemed like Greene was being mocked for a cultural ignorance they shared.

However insensitive the Wyoming establishment has been to working-class citizens' sensibilities and interests, it also has a sense of noblesse oblige. That sense of obligation inclines them to care about the general welfare of the state and work hard on behalf of those who are less fortunate. Their labors, moreover, seem to benefit the typical Wyomingite. Compared to other states, the citizens of Wyoming get more bang for their tax dollar. According to the Wyoming Taxpayers Association, a middle-class family of three receives $28,280 in public services a year, despite paying very little in taxes: an average of $3,770 annually. That figure includes property taxes. There is no income tax in Wyoming, and its sales tax is among the lowest in the nation.[24]

Public goods and services are a bargain in Wyoming because the old guard pushed for a tax on the extraction of minerals (natural gas, oil, and coal) back in the 1970s. After the state coffers hit a mere $80 in 1968, the state's Republican governor Stan Hathaway—who later served in the Ford administration—pushed for the new tax. Ever since then the state has been flush with money, a bit like the oil-rich nations of the Middle East.

And like many petrostates, Wyoming has provided generously for its people. Wyoming, for example, spends more on education than

---

[24] Janelle Frits, "State and Local Sales Tax Rates," Tax Foundation, February 3, 2022, https://taxfoundation.org/2022-sales-taxes/.

most states, including progressive ones like California, Maryland, and Washington.[25] One reason is that teachers are paid comparatively well, especially after adjusting for the cost of living. A typical teacher salary goes further in Wyoming than it does in 48 other states.[26] Wyoming's state university is also unusually accessible and affordable. The in-state tuition at the University of Wyoming is among the lowest in the nation, and practically everyone who applies is accepted. It's able to do so because, as a journalist at *Forbes* noted, the "Wyoming state government significantly underwrites the cost of public education to the tune of $15,000 per fully enrolled student per year."[27]

Thus, contrary to what critics of the Republican establishment would lead us to believe, Wyoming's establishment has been transferring billions from its mineral companies to everyone else—and has been doing so for decades. It's true that many in the old guard would prefer a more balanced tax structure, one less dependent on the boom-and-bust cycles of the energy sector. That would mean raising taxes on ordinary Wyomingites. But such views are born out of pragmatism, not greed. And given how little Wyomingites pay in taxes (and how much they get in return), such views seem like ones that Thomas Frank and his ilk might actually share.

To the extent the Wyoming establishment governed well, it certainly owed something to its talent and education. That conclusion is suggested by one important study of legislative effectiveness by Gerard Padro and James Snyder. Padro and Snyder set out to identify the variables that make for good lawmakers. Drawing on a survey that asked legislators, journalists, and lobbyists to assess the effectiveness of each member of the North Carolina House, Padro and Snyder found that lawyers make particularly effective legislators. As they concluded: "It is not surprising that lawyers are more effective, since legislators

[25] Chris Gilligan, "Which States Invest the Most in Their Students?," *U.S. News & World Report*, August 26, 2022, https://www.usnews.com/news/best-states/articles/2022-08-26/which-states-invest-the-most-in-their-students.

[26] "Comparison of Teacher Salaries Adjusted for Purchasing Power," https://kahlerfinancial.com/wp-content/uploads/2015/10/Teacher-Salary-Chart.pdf.

[27] James Marshall Crotty, "Wyoming Has the Lowest College Tuition in America," *Forbes*, December 31, 2014, https://www.forbes.com/sites/jamesmarshallcrotty/2014/12/31/wyoming-has-the-lowest-college-tuition-in-america-and-why-that-really-matters/?sh=768115df5de7.

make laws and lawyers have years of specialized training in the theory and application of law." "What is surprising," Padro and Snyder elaborated, "is the magnitude of the effect: being a lawyer appears to have a larger impact on effectiveness than being the chair of a powerful committee."[28] As Chapter 2 showed, lawyers are hardly equally represented among old and new guard legislators in Wyoming. While we were able to identify nine lawyers among establishment Republicans in the statehouse, we could not find a single lawyer among the new right legislators. If the new insurgents continue to advance, they are likely to drain the legislature of the skills and training that have contributed to successful lawmaking.

Wyoming's GOP establishment has done more than spread the state's wealth around and generally govern effectively: It has also been the custodian of a nobler form of politics. The old guard venerates the statehouse and its civic norms, especially civility and compromise. And, as we showed in Chapter 4, it also insists on keeping national issues of little relevance to day-to-day governance in Wyoming off the state agenda.

The members of Wyoming's Republican establishment are still fighting to protect its democratic traditions. To that end, many try to school the new insurgents. "They step out of line, and need to be corrected," Tom Walters, an "old head," told us. Walters says he tells the newcomers to criticize ideas, not people. "Don't say Tom has a bad idea," he tells the new types. Instead, "say, 'This is a bad idea for my community *because*—.'" Still, it's an uphill struggle. "When I was elected as a new member," Walters recalled, "you knew that you needed to keep your mouth shut and do a lot more listening than speaking so that you could learn." "The newer members do a lot more speaking and a lot less listening and learning."

With a bit of bemusement, the handful of Democrats in the statehouse observe this tutelage from afar. We sat down with Cathy Connolly, when she was the minority leader in the state house. Over beer in a quaint brewery in Laramie—Wyoming's only college town—Connolly told us that it has been "really interesting to watch

---

[28] Gerard Padró i Miquel and James Snyder, "Legislative Effectiveness and Legislative Careers," *Legislative Studies Quarterly* 31, no. 3 (2006): 358.

the Republican leadership . . . school their own." In the past that wasn't necessary. But after "this whole crop came in," Connolly recalled, that was "just being bombastic"—including one who likened the speaker to a demon—the old guard had to act. Now when newly elected members arrive in the legislature, the leadership tells them that their job isn't to bash the legislature, a message Connolly says has to be said "louder and louder" every year.

While Representatives Walters and Connolly are far apart politically, they both agree on the essential virtues that good legislators share, regardless of their politics. Good legislators should work hard, focus on state issues, find common ground where it exists, and never resort to personal attacks. As Connolly explained some of these norms with pride: "It is the expectation that everyone comes to their committee to work and work hard, and it doesn't make a difference what party you're from. It really doesn't."

Here again, the Cheneys exemplify both the virtues and vices of Wyoming's old guard. Dick Cheney may have exploited his political connections for personal gain, but, like Walters and Connolly, he also was a custodian of the deliberative norms that are the foundation of bipartisan governance. At times, Cheney's fellow Republicans were troubled by his reluctance to be more aggressive. As candidate for vice president in 2000, Cheney was expected to hurl some bombs at Joe Lieberman during their debate. The expectation was hardly unreasonable since it has long been a convention for presidential running mates to do some of this dirty work. But Cheney refused. The result was perhaps the most civil and thoughtful vice presidential debate in history. A typical observer noted that it was a "gentlemanly, civil affair."[29]

Cheney, for his part, took pride in his performance. "We never descended into personal attacks," he recalled with relish in his memoir.[30] To do so, even in a vice presidential debate where a little mudslinging is expected, not only would have been contrary to his own temperament

---

[29] Stephen F. Hayes, *Cheney: The Untold Story of America's Most Powerful and Controversial Vice President* (HarperCollins, 2007), 295.

[30] Dick Cheney, *In My Time: A Personal and Political Memoir* (Threshold Editions, 2011), 282.

and class-based cultural sensibilities—it would also mean turning against a Wyoming Republican establishment that he embodied so well.

* * * * *

MAGA-aligned elites, though, see a different problem with the Republican establishment from either defenders of liberal democracy or those concerned about class inequality. For them, the problem is not so much its alleged cravenness. Instead, it's simply not tough enough to defeat the "woke" left, which they believe is bent on destroying American civilization. This is why, they say, more party men should be shaped by the manly culture of the working class. After all, what is needed in this age of polarization are more fighters—not more well-mannered lawyers and bankers.

This growing sense of crisis among intellectuals on the Trump-aligned right has many sources. One is the new outrage media. Even before Trump's rise, Fox News and its ilk had long portrayed the left as a movement bent on destroying the American way of life.[31] A fear of civilizational collapse has also been cultivated by the intellectuals who defended Trump, particularly those at the Claremont Institute in California.

At the institute, none were more influential than Michael Anton. Prior to the election, Anton wrote his infamous essay in the *Claremont Review of Books* where he likened America's electoral choice between Hillary Clinton and Trump to the one faced by the passengers of Flight 93 on September 11th. Charging the cockpit, like voting for Trump, is risky, of course. But the alternative, Anton said, is far worse. As he memorably put it, "a Hillary Clinton presidency is Russian Roulette with a semi-auto. With Trump, at least you can spin the cylinder and take your chances."[32]

Over time, these intellectuals did more than just take their chances and hope for the best. They began to insist that Trump's willingness to fight an increasingly lawless enemy was a virtue. There was a logic to it. If one believes that progressives are bent on ruining American civilization

---

[31] Jeffrey M. Berry and Sarah Sobieraj, *The Outrage Media: Public Opinion, Media, and the New Incivility* (Oxford University Press, 2014), 47.

[32] Publius Decius Mus, "The Flight 93 Election," *Claremont Review of Books*, September 5, 2016, https://claremontreviewofbooks.com/digital/the-flight-93-election/.

by any means necessary, then empowering as many fearless strongmen as possible is a top priority. And, so, by 2020, Tom Klingenstein—a prominent MAGA donor and Claremont Institute chair—believed that Trump is "just what the doctor ordered" in "these revolutionary times." "I am almost prepared to say," Klingenstein wrote, "that having him is Providential."[33] This was not mere rhetorical flourish on Klingenstein's part: Note the capital "P."

After the January 6th insurrection, such intellectuals were left disappointed by the Republican professional class, especially its lawyers. They lacked any sense of "the revolutionary times" they were in, and thus couldn't summon the courage to fight an enemy bent on destroying America.

One lawyer who did stand his ground was the Claremont Institute's John Eastman. Infamously, Eastman concocted legal arguments for Trump that justified throwing out certified slates of electors. Eastman did so because he believed the election was stolen. In a legal memo to Trump, he wrote: "But this Election was Stolen by a strategic Democrat plan to systematically flout existing election laws for partisan advantage; we're no longer playing by Queensbury Rules, therefore."[34] As one conservative critic of the Eastman memo later wondered: "By what rules, then, are we playing?"[35]

The problem, as revolutionaries like Eastman see it, is that too many in the Republican establishment don't realize that they're fighting in an America more like the old West than in a well-ordered constitutional republic. After the Trump team failed to overturn the election, Eastman blamed it on the weakness of the Republican establishment. "They all spinelessly wouldn't do anything," he complained.[36]

---

[33] Thomas Klingenstein, "A Man vs. a Movement," *Real Clear Politics*, October 13, 2020, https://www.realclearpolitics.com/video/2020/10/13/claremont_institute_chairman_thomas_klingenstein_trump_2020_a_man_vs_a_movement.html.

[34] See Eastman January 6th memo, https://www.justsecurity.org/wp-content/uploads/2022/06/january-6-clearinghouse-john-eastman-six-page-jan-3-memo-on-jan-6-scenario.pdf.

[35] Jospeh M. Bessette, "A Critique of the Eastman Memos," *Claremont Review of Books*, Fall 2021, https://claremontreviewofbooks.com/critique-eastman-memos/.

[36] Mary Papenfuss, "'Coup Memo' Attorney Blasts 'Spineless' GOP Lawmakers Who Refused To Jettison Election," HuffPost, Oct 30, 2021, https://www.huffpost.com/entry/lauren-windsor-john-eastman-trump-spineless-election_n_617dd8fee4b079111a65aada.

It is, thus, of little surprise that the Claremont Institute has been eager to build a more manly party, one anchored not in spineless lawyers but in rugged cowboys. To that end, the institute created a program for "Sheriff Fellows." In the summer of 2021 an inaugural group of eight sheriffs—mostly from far-flung rural counties—arrived in posh Huntington Beach, California, to reflect on how these lawmen can best maintain American liberty. The scene captured some elite Republicans' newfound infatuation with working-class strongmen, where those with doctorates in political philosophy could enlighten and dine with country sheriffs in 10-gallon hats. It was a bit reminiscent of some affluent liberals in the late 1960s who delighted in mingling with Black Power militants at their cocktail parties. For some elites, flirting with revolution by brushing up against strongmen from the lower classes seemed intoxicating.

To celebrate strongmen, the Claremont Institute program also included a screening of John Ford's classic western *The Man Who Killed Liberty Valance*.[37] Ford's film contrasts two archetypal characters. One is Ransom Stoddard (played by Jimmy Stewart), a lawyer who represents the professional class and the rule-bound civilization it governs. The other is Tom Doniphon (played by John Wayne), a virtuous strongman governed by an honor culture. Ford's film reminds us of the need for men like Doniphon in places not governed by the rule of law. In an early scene, Stoddard, who states he is an "attorney-at-law, duly licensed for the territories," approaches a frontier town in an unidentified western state, only to be robbed and beaten by an outlaw gang. The gang tears up Stoddard's law books, before he is rescued by Doniphon. After Stoddard recovers, he insists that these bandits must be tried and prosecuted. But Doniphon replies that such legal justice isn't possible on the frontier: "Out here a man settles his own problems."

Thus, when Eastman and his ilk complain about spineless lawyers, they are expressing a longing for a party led by men like Doniphon rather than Stoddard, at least until the rule of law can be restored. What

---

37 Jessica Pishko, "Here Is the Secret 'Sheriff Fellowship' Curriculum from the Country's Most Prominent MAGA Think Tank," *Slate*, September 21, 2022, https://slate.com/news-and-politics/2022/09/claremont-institute-secret-sheriff-fellowship-curriculum-revealed.html.

is needed are men who are governed by an honor culture, men who will restore order and justice to a lawless America. What is needed are modern-day cowboys.

The Wyoming GOP—as well as those in plenty of other western states—did send some fearless cowboys to Washington, DC, on January 6th. One was the chair of the state party, Frank Eathorne. He was spotted on the Capitol grounds, talking into a portable radio and carrying a backpack.[38]

Eathorne embodies the new rugged party leader, the sort Eastman believes are necessary to save America. He even looks like a modern-day John Wayne. Handsome, strong, and always donning his cowboy hat, Eathorne towers over most other men in the Wyoming GOP.

He also has strong working-class bona fides. Before climbing the ranks of the state party, Eathorne worked as a Terminix pest exterminator and a police officer in Worland, a Wyoming town with fewer than 6,000 residents. As a younger man, he competed in rodeos and as a bull rider.

Like so many in his world, Eathorne has a messy personal life. As a police officer in Worland, he was caught receiving oral sex in his patrol car during the midnight shift. Most recently, his wife of many years divorced him for cheating on her.[39] And he has been threatening, too. Eathorne was charged, credibly it seems, with attempted sexual assault. He allegedly barged drunk and armed into the apartment of a young dispatcher, demanding sex. Eventually, Eathorne was turned away.[40]

Such brazenness is appealing to those elite Republicans who have been radicalized by today's polarized politics. For those who really believe they are in an existential battle to save America, then summoning an army of men like Eathorne is necessary, even if a bit unseemly. Unlike

[38] Andrew Rossi, "Wyoming GOP Chairman Frank Eathorne Spotted Among January 6th Rioters at U.S. Capitol," *Big Horn Basin Media*, June 1, 2022, https://mybighornbasin.com/wyoming-gop-chairman-frank-eathorne-spotted-amongst-jan-6-rioters-at-us-capitol/.

[39] Rod Miller, "Hypocrisy in the Wyoming GOP, the Sequel," *Cowboy State Daily*, November 18, 2022, https://cowboystatedaily.com/2022/11/18/rod-miller-hypocrisy-in-the-wyoming-gop-the-sequel/.

[40] Victoria Eavis and Rone Tempest, "Wyoming GOP Chairman Quietly Assumed Power as Party Fractured," *WyoFile*, May 20, 2022, https://wyofile.com/wyo-gop-chairman-quietly-assumed-power-as-party-fractured/.

the lawyers, men like Eathorne are willing to storm the cockpit—and the Capitol. That's why the chair of the Claremont Institute concluded: "Trump is the perfect man for these times, not all times, perhaps not most times, but these times." Later, he added: "In war, you must make a stand. For that, we need strong men."[41]

From the Claremont Institute's point of view, the only real class-related problem with middle America is its elevated body mass index (BMI). Recently, one of its writers lamented that conservatives can't win the war against "woke" liberals unless middle America gets in shape. "As conservative BMI goes, so goes the movement—and America," he concluded. High BMIs, after all, make it hard to storm the Capitol, with all those marble steps. The article included detailed instructions for getting in shape, as well as this bit of encouragement: "Get off your ass. Pump some iron. Build muscle and, more importantly, in doing [so] build the strength of character that forms the backbone of a prosperous republic.[42]

There is much to criticize in the radical turn the Claremont Institute and other conservatives have taken. Many have commented on their absurd apocalypticism and support for dangerous conspiracy theories.[43] Less noticed has been their unwitting embrace of a right-wing version of identity politics.

What these MAGA-aligned intellectuals don't seem to notice are the commonalities between the new guard types and those on the left. As previous chapters have shown, there is a "woke" right in Wyoming. Identity politics isn't just a left-wing thing. That's because both left- and right-wing identity politics share a family resemblance. Like its counterpart on the right, the "woke" left has often frustrated governing liberals who are more interested in addressing common problems rather than expressing identity.[44]

---

[41]   Quoted in Randal Hendrickson, "It's Manly Man Summer at the Claremont Institute," *The Constitutionalist*, August 4, 2022, https://theconstitutionalist.org/2022/08/04/its-manly-man-summer-at-the-claremont-institute/.

[42]   Bill C., "Get Fit for Service," *The American Mind*, November 11, 2021, https://americanmind.org/salvo/get-fit-for-service/.

[43]   See, for example, Laura K. Field, "What the Hell Happened to the Claremont Institute?," *Bulwark*, July 13, 2021, https://www.thebulwark.com/what-the-hell-happened-to-the-claremont-institute/.

[44]   See, for example, Hersh, *Politics Is for Power*.

These commonalities have been obscured because some of the sharpest accounts of identity politics have regarded it as largely a preoccupation of the left. One prominent theory, for example, says that identity politics grew out of academia, before it spread out into the American left more generally. Helen Pluckrose and James Lindsay's book *Cynical Theories* traces identity politics to French critical theory back in the 1960s. It was a germ, they say, that was injected into American universities, before it eventually spread and corrupted our nation's liberal traditions. A similar analysis is told by Yascha Mounk in his recent, much-discussed book *The Identity Trap*.

Even on its face, it seems unlikely that American politics is downstream from French political theory. It simply grants too much power to intellectuals. But the problem with such origin stories is deeper still: They can't explain why conservatives are embracing identity politics, much less why it looks so similar to its progressive rival.

To address that problem, it seems sensible to assume that this age of identity politics has some common sources, even if the leftist version has been shaped by currents from academia. One explanation might be that polarization and secularization are reshaping Americans' spiritual lives in ways that encourage identity politics. As Americans have sorted themselves into like-minded communities, it creates an opportunity for activists and candidates to acquire political power by making ever more strident demands. At the same time, though, secularization is reshaping Americans' quest for meaning and belonging. As Americans have drifted from their religious communities altogether, they may be trying to transform their parties and workplaces into the churches they don't attend anymore. Thus, perhaps these places are serving as a substitute for religious institutions. David French, a *New York Times* columnist and close observer of the MAGA right, believes that has happened to his fellow conservatives: "They have religious zeal, but they lack religious community. So they find their band of brothers and sisters in the Trump movement."[45]

---

[45] David French, "The Rage and Joy of MAGA America," *New York Times*, July 6, 2023, https://www.nytimes.com/2023/07/06/opinion/maga-america-trump. html?smid=nytcore-ios-share&referringSource=articleShare.

In the 1960s, the drift from religious communities began because of individualistic currents within Christianity. "Across Protestant and Catholic religious life," concludes sociologist Andrew Cherlin, "the spirituality of seeking was not about laws or doctrines but about finding a style of spirituality that made you feel good."[46] These changes prepared the new right for a more expressive, identity politics. Much like this revamped Christianity, the end of the new politics is all about expressing oneself in ways that feel gratifying, rather than being constrained by and integrated into an institution.

Now the subculture that has grown up around the new right in Wyoming feels as if it's drifting even further from traditional Christian norms. At the Trump rally we attended in Casper, for example, we saw many "Fuck Biden" flags and T-shirts. The prevalence of this profanity—and its public acceptance—reminded us of the drift of the American right from the church. Those who stormed the Capitol also bore some of these same post-Christian markers. One was the "QAnon Shaman," dressed like a Viking conqueror, wearing war paint and a bison-horned headdress. Tattooed to his chest are images of Thor's hammer and what seems to be the Norse tree Yggdrasil.[47] Like so many of those who fell into the QAnon cult, the QAnon Shaman is someone who sought and found a new religion. And in his case, secularization on the right sometimes seems like a drift back to the pagan world that Christianity was supposed to replace once and for all.

While the insurgents in Wyoming don't worship Norse gods, their behavior and rhetoric sometimes suggest that their sojourn into the wilds of Wyoming politics is a spiritual quest. A good example is Anthony Bouchard, the first to declare his candidacy against Liz Cheney. During the candidate debate for Cheney's seat, Bouchard recalled the moment of his political awakening in language that would be familiar to born-again Christians: "Obamacare is . . . one of the things that got

---

[46] Andrew Cherlin, *The Marriage-Go Round: The State of Marriage and the Family in America Today* (Knopf Doubleday Publishing Group, 2010), 105–8, 113–15.

[47] Tom Birkett, "US Capitol Riot: The Myths Behind the Tattoos Worn by 'QAnon Shaman' Jake Angeli," *ABC News*, January 13, 2021, https://www.abc.net.au/news/2021-01-13/us-capitol-riot-myths-behind-the-tattoos-worn-by-jake-angeli/13053600.

me awake."[48] Anthony, it seems, was blind, but now he sees. Others, explicitly say their party is their religion. One party member explained: "Your party is like your religion. . . . You don't just join any church. You go to a particular one, because what they believe in aligns with what you believe."[49] This analysis was affirmed by a state lawmaker who is extremely conservative but nonetheless stays aloof from the new guard, saying with irritation and dismay: "It's a cult! A religious thing. If you deviate you get expelled." In fact, many of the new conservative activists moved to Wyoming from out of state precisely because they saw it as a conservative Mecca, a place untouched by progressive values.

In this respect, they seem quite similar to social justice activists on America's most progressive campuses. Like the Puritans of old, their adopted homelands are supposed to be a new Jerusalem, a holy land untouched by the moral pollution of the larger society. Yet that ambition breeds a fear that these islands of holiness are threatened by witches. And because these demons are hard to see, everyone must be on guard and purge those who seem the least bit suspicious.

Seeking spiritual identity in politics has also inverted the relationship between religion and politics in the modern right. In the twentieth century, conservative movements—from anti-communism to the campaign against abortion—have been sustained by Catholic and Protestant churches. That allowed these believers to express their religiosity in sacred spaces apart from politics, which, in turn, helped them to instrumentalize their activism. Catholics and Protestants, for example, put aside their deep theological differences to fight for fetal rights. And both groups often toned down their religious expression in the public square by using secular arguments. They did so because they didn't join the pro-life movement simply to express their identity as Christians— they joined it to change opinion and policies. And they understood

---

[48] C-SPAN, "Campaign 2022: Wyoming U.S. House Republican Debate," June 30, 2022, https://www.c-span.org/video/?521447-1/wyoming-us-house-republican-debate.

[49] Nick Reynolds, "In Rebuke of Wyoming GOP, Natrona County Republicans Oppose Several Conservative-Led Initiatives," *Casper Star-Tribune*, July 24, 2019, https://trib.com/news/state-and-regional/govt-and-politics/in-rebuke-of-wyoming-gop-natrona-county-republicans-oppose-several/article_715563ed-d97d-559f-a393-1569a0aefa1c.html.

that to be persuasive, they have to frame their cause in language that's compelling to their fellow citizens.[50]

But the new right is quite different: It wants to find a spiritual identity and community *in* politics. As a consequence, its activists can find no civic world below politics in which they can make a spiritual life. Either they don't attend church at all or the churches they do attend have become so co-opted by conservative politics that they have effectively become auxiliary party organizations. A harrowing and poignant example of such a transformation was recently published by Christian Republican activist and *New York Times* columnist David French. When his family became members of the small Presbyterian Church in America in 2004, it was a denomination where he "never heard political messages from the pulpit" and "worshiped alongside Democratic friends." But when he came out against Trump in 2016, the good will and political ecumenism began to evaporate, prompting his family eventually to leave. This led in 2024 to him being invited by some in his former religious community to speak publicly about the difficulty churches were facing in such polarized times. Before he could, however, French was nastily denounced, and the event was canceled. Opposing Trump seemed un-Christian.[51]

Secularization aside, the new identity politics grows out of a long tradition of American populism. Like populists of old, identitarians on the left and right share a deep distrust toward those in power. Both assume that society is organized to serve the interests of the powerful, making a sharp Manichean contrast between the virtuous people and a corrupt elite. That belief, in turn, encourages conspiracy theory, especially the idea that a corrupt elite is plotting to destroy the people, rightly understood. For the left, it's the "new Jim Crow"; for the right, it's the "deep state." And each tends to believe that they are the real majority, obstructed by the machinations of their enemies: For the right, elections are rigged by Democrats; for the left, voting is suppressed by Republicans.

---

[50] Jon A. Shields, *The Democratic Virtues of the Christian Right* (Princeton University Press, 2009), 33–39.

[51] David French, "The Day My Old Church Canceled Me Was a Very Sad Day," *New York Times*, June 9, 2024.

Like populists everywhere, conservatives and progressives who are drawn to the new identity politics also see themselves as outsiders, even when they become insiders. On college campuses, activists always call themselves "marginalized," even though they tend to dominate student politics and shape the public culture. Similarly, Wyoming's new insurgents invoke the same metaphor, distinguishing between a corrupt and privileged core and an unjustly dispossessed periphery. They too always see themselves as marginalized, though they don't explicitly use the "m" word. Chuck Gray, a Trumpy legislator and now Wyoming secretary of state, whose father owned a Wyoming radio station, always cast himself as an outsider fighting the "insiders."

These outsiders also share the idea that people from below have a clearer insight into our society than those who are more powerful. Here again, progressives who embrace identity politics give it a different name than their conservative counterparts. They call it "standpoint epistemology." And while the term itself comes from academia, the notion resonates with the broad tradition of American populism.

Outsiders are thought to enjoy special sight partly because their removal from centers of power connects them to everyday life. And it's these experiences that impart critical knowledge, not credentials in universities far removed from common life. Again, progressives give this populist idea a name conservatives don't use. They call it "lived experience." But such superficial differences shouldn't obscure what they have in common.

We do not mean to suggest that today's identity politics is like all past expressions of populism. At times, populist movements have been more firmly anchored in specific causes and didn't seem so consumed with identity. The agrarian populists of the late nineteenth century, for example, had a major influence over the federal regulatory state and were willing to create broad coalitions to achieve those ends.[52]

Today's movements, though, sometimes seem like they can never be assuaged because they're not rooted in well-defined interests. A frustrated Tom Walters, an establishment voice in Wyoming's legislature, pointed to this problem, even as he acknowledged that the old party

---

[52] See Elizabeth Sanders, *Roots of Reform: Farmers, Workers, and the American State, 1877–1917* (University of Chicago Press, 1999).

was arguably too beholden to a handful of corporate interests. "The Ag interests, the large ranchers, for a long time, sure, they recruited the candidates that they thought would be sympathetic to their causes. . . . The oil interests, the mineral interests, did the exact same thing," he told us. But at least they had interests. "And now we have a group of people that have no interests," he continued, "but want to be the voice of something. And I don't know what that something is."

College administrators face a similar challenge when confronted with social justice activists. Like Walters, there is nothing they could ever do to satisfy these outraged parties. As John McWhorter has described the new left: "What they are after is not money or power, but sheer purpose."[53] In both cases, the point of politics is the construction and maintenance of identities that are, by definition, outside and against the establishment. They must always be outsiders, forever marginalized and victims. This is the tendency of populists, generally. As Bill Galston has observed, "populism plunges societies into an endless series of moralized, zero-sum conflicts."[54]

Even so, we also don't mean to suggest that the new identity politics on the right is just like its progressive rival. There are many important differences. For one thing, they have taken root in different institutions. On the right, cancel culture is most powerful in the Republican Party; and, on the left, it's most influential in universities. That's because cancel culture thrives in places that are ideologically homogeneous. One reason congressional Democrats have avoided bitter purge campaigns—like the one that deposed Kevin McCarthy—is that the party is simply too diverse. It's composed of a wider range of interests and social groups. As Ezra Klein has emphasized, fewer than half of Democrats self-identify as liberal, while three-quarters of Republicans identify as conservatives. "As a result," Klein observed, "winning the Democratic primary means winning liberal whites in New Hampshire

---

53 John McWhorter, *Woke Racism: How a New Religion Has Betrayed Black America* (Portfolio, 2021), 40.

54 William Galston, "The Populist Challenge to Liberal Democracy," *Journal of Democracy* 29, no. 2 (2018): 13.

and traditionalist blacks in South Carolina."[55] That keeps the desire to purify the party in check.

A more obvious difference is that populism is married to different programmatic agendas on the right and left. This is in the nature of populism, which tends to attach itself to different host ideologies. As Cas Mudde reminds us, this is why populism "seldom exists in a pure form." It is a "thin" ideology that needs other elements to establish its ends.[56]

The final difference is more painfully obvious: there is no analogue to Trump on the left. It's hard to overstate the significance of that difference. Additionally, the right has had more success infiltrating political institutions, such as parties, legislatures, and the White House, while the left has enjoyed more success remaking the nation's intellectual and cultural institutions, especially universities and newsrooms. As a consequence, though, governing liberals are far more influential in the Democratic Party than governing conservatives are in the GOP. This seems true throughout the Western world more generally. As Anne Applebaum has observed, "although the cultural power of the authoritarian left is growing, the only modern *clerics* who have attained real *political* power in western democracies—the only ones operating inside governments, participating in ruling coalitions, guiding important political parties—are members of movements that we are accustomed to calling the 'right.'"[57]

These institutional differences seem connected to the class divide that often separates white liberals and conservatives. In the Democratic Party, those most taken with identity politics tend to be the

---

[55] Ezra Klein, "Why Democrats Still Have to Appeal to the Center, but Republicans Don't," *New York Times*, January 24, 2020, https://www.nytimes.com/2020/01/24/opinion/sunday/democrats-republicans-polarization.html; see also Matt Grossman and David A. Hopkins, *Asymmetrical Politics: Ideological Republicans and Group Interest Democrats* (Oxford University Press, 2016).

[56] Cas Mudde, *Populism: A Very Short Introduction* (Oxford University Press, 2017), 6–7.

[57] Anne Applebaum, *Twilight of Democracy: The Seductive Lure of Authoritarianism* (Anchor Books, 2021), 19; see also, Francis Fukuyama, "Liberalism and Its Discontents: The Challenges of the Left and the Right," *American Purpose*, October 5, 2020.

most affluent, educated whites; and they are often at odds with more centrist working- and middle-class Blacks and Latinos. While the former dominates elite cultural institutions, the latter has moderated the Democratic Party by elevating moderate candidates, like Joe Biden and New York mayor, Eric Adams. Identity politics in the Republican Party, meanwhile, is sustained by a much broader base of white voters who often are reacting against cultural elites on the left.

* * * * *

In this chapter, we've argued that critics of the Republican establishment miss their marks, although to varying degrees.

The Wyoming story should at least temper the view that the Republican establishment has simply been Trump's lapdog. This is not to suggest that we should be sanguine about a return of the GOP to its old self, either in Wyoming or elsewhere. As many others have emphasized, the Republican Party has been drifting away from a responsible governing conservatism since the 1990s.[58] While we are not especially sanguine about its return, we are impressed by the many Republicans we met working to revive it. And the fact that it is still fighting for the soul of the party in the nation's reddest state should give liberal critics of the new right some modicum of hope for the party's future.

Our time in Wyoming leaves us more skeptical of progressive critics of the Republican establishment. Unless the Wyoming GOP is an unusually publicly spirited oddity, its example suggests that members of the Republican establishment more broadly are not as craven as the left imagines. If it were otherwise, it would be hard to explain why so many working-class citizens from our home blue state of California are flooding into nearby states that are governed by Republicans. As the political

---

[58] See, for example, Barbara Sinclair, *Party Wars: Polarization and the Politics of National Policy Making* (University of Oklahoma Press, 2006); Nicole Hemmer, *Messengers of the Right: Conservative Media and the Transformation of American Politics* (University of Pennsylvania Press, 2018); Brian Rosenfeld, *Talk Radio's America: How an Industry Took Over a Political Party That Took Over the United States* (Harvard University Press, 2019); Nicole Hemmer, *Partisans: The Conservative Revolutionaries Who Remade American Politics in the 1990s* (Basic Books, 2022). The decline of moderate and center-left Republicans is an older trend. See Geoffrey Kabaservice, *Rule and Ruin: The Downfall of Moderation and the Destruction of the Republican Party, from Eisenhower to the Tea Party* (Oxford University Press, 2013).

scientist Ken Miller found in his careful study of California and Texas politics: "Large numbers of middle- and working-class Americans concluded that it was easier to find a job, buy a home, support a family, and build a future in Texas than in California or other blue states."[59] Many of our own working-class relatives have been part of this migration.

And contrary to what some conservative intellectuals suggest, the problem with today's right is not the unwillingness of the Republican establishment to forcefully challenge identity politics. A far greater concern is the new right's effort to transform the GOP into a woke party. Needless to say, genuine enemies of identity politics should not seek the remaking of the GOP's state parties into right-wing versions of Oberlin College.

---

[59] Kenneth P. Miller, *Texas vs. California: A History of Their Struggle for the Future of America* (Oxford University Press, 2020), 249.

CONCLUSION:
THE FUTURE OF THE GOP

As this book goes to press, Wyoming's Republican civil war still rages. The party's rival political action committees (Freedom Caucus and Wyoming Caucus) raised roughly similar sums leading up to the 2024 primaries.[1] Some $4.5 million was spent on the primaries, an unusually high amount for Wyoming.[2] Well funded and ready for battle, each side scored some significant victories.

The establishment successfully ousted a few MAGA-aligned incumbents in the Wyoming House. One was Jeanette Ward, a self-described political refugee from Illinois.[3] Elected in 2022, Ward quickly earned a reputation for being among the most vocal members of the new right. Her opponent, Julie Jarvis, ran as a classic old guard candidate, accusing Ward and her ilk of creating a "political circus" that is unconcerned with

---

[1] The Freedom Caucus raised $179,875, while the Wyoming Caucus raised $199,464. See Chris Clements, "Receipts Show Wyoming GOP Groups Spent Less During the General Election," Wyoming Public Radio, November 25, 2024, https://www.wyomingpublicmedia.org/politics-government/2024-11-25/receipts-show-wyoming-gop-groups-spent-less-during-the-general-election.

[2] Equality State Policy Center, *In a High Spending Primary, Do Winners Spend More?*, Wyoming 2024 Primary Election Campaign Finance Report (Equality State Policy Center, October 2024).

[3] Brendan LaChance, "Candidate Questionnaire: Jeanette Ward for House District 57," *Oil City News*, July 1, 2022.

"how decisions impact local people."[4] Jarvis won handily, capturing 57 percent of the vote. Landon Brown—the outspoken Cheney supporter profiled throughout this book—also held onto his seat. Brown narrowly survived a fierce challenge from Exie Brown, a small business owner and retired Air Force veteran.

Overall, though, candidates aligned with the Freedom Caucus had more success—and they continued to reshape the class profile of the Wyoming legislature. Tom Walters, the long-serving stalwart of the old guard, was defeated by Jayme Lien, a high school graduate whose husband works in Wyoming's coal mines. Likewise, Ember Oakley, a county attorney, lost her seat to Joel Guggenmos, a new right candidate who runs a small business installing showers and hardwood floors. If these trends continue, the legislature will continue to look more like most Wyomingites, though it may also lose all of its lawyers.

These successes will give the Freedom Caucus the narrowest of majorities in the House once new members are seated in 2025.[5] According to one analysis by Wyoming Public Radio, the caucus will have at least 33 seats in the 62-member House. The precise number is always difficult to calculate since the Wyoming Freedom Caucus doesn't publish its members' names. Wyoming Public Radio cobbled together information from voting records, campaign finance reports, and official endorsements to reach its estimate.[6] Proof of the new guard's capture of the statehouse, though, is the ascendance of its members into positions of leadership. In the House, four were elected to leadership positions, including Chip Neiman as speaker. The Senate, meanwhile, opted for a mix of new and old guard Republicans.

In short, the elections of 2024 were historic in Wyoming. Not only did the new guard seize control over the House but its elevation is also

---

[4] See campaign video, "Julie Jarvis HD57 Campaign Launch," YouTube, 3 min., 17 sec., https://www.youtube.com/watch?v=0-opGIRKZj4.

[5] Maggie Mullens, "Wyoming Freedom Caucus Gains Power, but November Will Determine Statehouse Control," WyoFile, August 21, 2024, https://wyofile.com/wyoming-freedom-caucus-gains-power-but-november-will-determine-statehouse-con trol/.

[6] Chris Clements, "Majority Control: Wyoming Freedom Caucus Grabs State House Power," Wyoming Public Radio, November 15, 2024, https://www.wyomingp ublicmedia.org/politics-government/2024-11-15/majority-control-wyoming-freedom -caucus-grabs-state-house-power.

a first in the nation. No legislature in any American state or in the Congress has ever been controlled outright by the Freedom Caucus. After the 2024 elections, the Wyoming journalist Maggie Muller observed: "Wyoming is poised to become the first state in the nation to see a Freedom Caucus take the statehouse reins."[7]

As expected, the new right's agenda includes mostly symbolic measures, like invalidating drivers' licenses issued to undocumented immigrants in other states and tightening election security. "We're going to unwoke the state," explained the incoming speaker pro tem.[8] That ambition, though, will be resisted by a well-organized group of establishment Republicans and their thinning allies in the Democratic Party, all of whom regard these obsessions as a distraction from real problems.

The long-term future of the old guard is still hard to see. Perhaps their numbers will continue to dwindle slowly with each passing election, making them effectively a permanent minority party within the legislature. Even if that comes to pass, though, there will at least be a strong incentive for the new guard to take governing seriously. After all, it's hard to see how this new establishment will be able to maintain control over the legislature in the long run, if they simply refuse to govern. What's more clear is that Wyoming politics should be watched closely. Since it is the first red state in the nation to be captured by the new right, it may serve as a window into the future of the American right.

Meanwhile, in red states across the nation, civil wars like Wyoming's are going strong. In these places Republican establishments have been resisting the Trumpification of their party, resulting in fierce intra-party struggles in Colorado, Idaho, Nebraska, South Dakota, South Carolina, and Texas, among others.[9] And, like Wyoming, the new insurgents tend

---

7 Maggie Mullers, "With Leadership Victory, Wyoming Freedom Caucus Poised for Nation's First Statehouse Takeover," Wyofile, November 23, 2024, https://wyofil e.com/with-leadership-victory-wyoming-freedom-caucus-poised-for-nations-first-stat ehouse-takeover/.

8 David W. Chen, "How the Freedom Caucus Rose to Power in Wyoming," *New York Times*, December 26, 2024.

9 Jasper Scherer, "Texas Runoff Yields No Clear Winner Among GOP's Warring Factions, Setting Stage for Power Struggle," *Texas Tribune*, May 30, 2024; Michelle Goldberg, "The Gay-Bashing Email Splitting Colorado's Republican Party," *New York*

to dominate state parties and rural counties but are weaker in the legislature. As best as we can tell, the philosophical fault lines look the same, too. In deep red South Dakota, for example, the insurgents call the old guard "fake Republicans," while the establishment defends civility and everyday governance.[10] Similarly, Reese Boyd, the chair of a county party in South Carolina, complained that the new insurgents "want to call everybody that they disagree with a RINO."[11] And, in a number of states, governing conservatives have formed alliances with their fellow Democrats, much as they have in Wyoming.[12]

Regardless of their outcomes, one thing is clear: the insurgency can't be reversed, not fully. The new activists, demanding more power and representation for working-class voters in rural communities, aren't going anywhere. That faction looks like it will be around for some time, even if it doesn't manage to take over the party. What's more, a more diverse party is in itself a good thing and certainly not to be lamented.

The challenge for traditionalists, then, is to steer more of the new insurgents away from empty performance art and sabotage to an interest in governance. That may be happening, at least here and there.

Times, June 10, 2024; Margery Beck, "The Nebraska GOP Is Rejecting all Republican Congressional Incumbents in Tuesday's Primary Election," Associated Press, May 13, 2024; Joshua Haiar, "Republican Factions Fighting for Control of the Party in Tuesday's Primary Election," *South Dakota Searchlight*, June 1, 2024; Audrey Dutton, "What Idaho's Republican Primary Tells Us About America's Culture Wars," *ProPublica*, June 4, 2024; Anne Applebaum, "Is Tennessee a Democracy?," *Atlantic*, July 18, 2023; Nick Reynolds, "Hardliners Defeated Among Internal SC Republican Party Feuds," *The Post and Courier*, May 4, 2024.

[10] Haiar, "Republican Factions Fighting for Control."

[11] Stephen Fowler, "What GOP Infighting in South Carolina Can (and Can't) Tell Us About 2024," National Public Radio, February 22, 2024, https://www.npr.org/2024/02/22/1232818164/south-carolina-gop-infighting-rnc-donald-trump-horry-county.

[12] Yereth Rosen, "In New Bipartisan Alaska Senate Majority of 17, Members Vow Compromise and Consensus," *Alaska Public Media*, November 29, 2022, https://alaskapublic.org/2022/11/29/in-new-bipartisan-alaska-senate-majority-of-17-members-vow-compromise-and-consensus/; Morgan Trau, "Statehouse 'Coup'—Ohio GOP Bitterly Divided by Deal with Democrats to Elect House Speaker," *Ohio Capital Journal*, January 9, 2023, https://ohiocapitaljournal.com/2023/01/09/statehouse-coup-ohio-gop-bitterly-divided-by-deal-with-democrats-to-elect-house-speaker/; J. David Goodman, "Long Before Impeachment, G.O.P. Rifts Were Growing in Texas," *New York Times*, May 28, 2023, https://www.nytimes.com/2023/05/28/us/texas-republicans-ken-paxton-legislature.html.

But it's not just the new guard that needs to change. If the Republican Party is genuinely going to become the party of working-class Americans, then it needs to develop an agenda that serves them better. The vacuity of conservative identity politics should not obscure the real interests and grievances of the working class. It has benefited least from our global economy. It's also true that various interests—like doctors, pharmaceutical companies, and bankers—have used the levers of government to redistribute wealth upward. As the "liberal-tarian" thinkers Brink Lindsey and Steven Teles—both of whom are no fans of populism—acknowledge, "the powerful have rigged the economic game in their favor." They conclude: "Elites have conspired to hoard opportunity, manipulate the rules and their control of the political system to generate wealth for themselves, even as living standards for everyone else stagnate or decline."[13] Tackling this opportunity hoarding should be a top priority for the party.

Making a party for the working class, though, will require more than technocratic policy adjustments. It also means sharing real power with working-class citizens. After all, politics is not just a contest over the distribution of material resources—it's also about respect and dignity. At times, our interviews reminded us of that basic truth. When we chatted with Freddy Flores, a working-class transplant from the Bronx, she recalled attending Laramie County party meetings. At those meetings, she said, it was made clear that she was not part of the Republican "club." The leadership, she said, "welcomed our money and our volunteer hours, but not our input." And so when a bomb-throwing, anti-establishment figure like Anthony Bouchard emerged, Freddy saw someone who shared her sense that those in charge were corrupt. This is the problem with conservative noblesse oblige: While it encourages charity toward the less fortunate, it never doubts its right to rule over them.

In the absence of those declining institutions that were once centers of working-class power—especially unions and local political machines—it seems likely that working-class activists like Freddy will

---

[13] Brink Lindsey and Steven M. Teles, *The Captured Economy: How the Powerful Enrich Themselves, Slow Down Growth, and Increase Inequality* (Oxford University Press, 2019), 4.

keep gravitating to candidates like Bouchard. Today's conservative identity politics has filled the vacuum of that institutional decline. What's desperately needed, then, is either the revitalization of these fading institutions or the development of new centers of political power for working-class Americans.

At a minimum, the Republican "club" (as Freddy put it) will need to change in ways that will allow it to co-opt the Bouchards of the world. And in some respects, local parties in places like Wyoming are the rarest of American institutions: places where upper- and working-class Americans find themselves side by side, working in the same civic and political spaces. Time will tell if they become something more than sites of class resentment and conflict.

A conservative party, broadly representative of the working class, also can't reduce politics to technocratic concerns. Moral issues are inescapable and have an important place in politics. In the wake of the *Dobbs* decision, state legislatures have been wrangling over abortion policy, raising difficult questions over the scope of human rights.[14] That's as it should be.

Not only are issues like abortion important in and of themselves; they are also better at engaging citizens in politics than more technocratic ones. Issues like abortion, after all, stir moral passions. As American politics has become more centered on moral and cultural issues in recent decades, voter turnout has increased.[15] Participation in other forms of political expression, such as rallies and demonstrations, seems to be rising as well.[16]

---

[14] See, for example, Mitch Smith, "In a Contentious Lawmaking Season, Red States Got Redder and Blue Ones Bluer," *New York Times*, June 4, 2023, https://www.nytimes.com/2023/06/04/us/state-legislatures-opposite-agendas.html.

[15] Monican Potts, "Turnout Was High Again. Is This the New Normal?," *FiveThirtyEight*, November 15, 2022, https://fivethirtyeight.com/features/turnout-was-high-again-is-this-the-new-normal/; Pew Research Center, "Turnout Soared in 2020 as Nearly Two-Thirds of Eligible U.S. Voters Cast Ballots for President," January 28, 2021, https://www.pewresearch.org/short-reads/2021/01/28/turnout-soared-in-2020-as-nearly-two-thirds-of-eligible-u-s-voters-cast-ballots-for-president/.

[16] See, for example, Erica Chenowith et al., "The Trump Years Launched the Biggest Sustained Protest Movement in U.S. History. It's Not Over," *Washington Post*, February 8, 2021, https://www.washingtonpost.com/politics/2021/02/08/trump-years-launched-biggest-sustained-protest-movement-us-history-its-not-over/.

And as participation has swelled, our democracy has become more inclusive, bringing in Americans who have been comparatively marginal to our public life. In 2020, for example, turnout not only increased among Asians, Latinos, and younger Americans; it also rose among non-college-educated whites.[17] Voting aside, working-class whites are also more engaged in the life of the Republican Party. In Wyoming, they are better represented in both the state party and legislature. Its experience seems typical. A recent study of Republican state legislators found that those with lower levels of education were more likely to be newcomers affiliated with the Tea Party.[18]

We also don't mean to suggest that parties should never discipline its members when they stray too far from their core principles. As sociologists have long observed, all groups have boundaries; otherwise, there is no group. And because all groups have boundaries, there are also lines that can be crossed; hence, all groups can be betrayed. That means that as long as there are groups, there will always be sellouts.[19]

In other words, Republicans in name only (RINOs) are real. It's reasonable for activists and leaders in the GOP to worry about them. This is perhaps particularly so in one-party states where the only viable path into political power is the Republican Party, outside of a couple of small, blue enclaves. Those conditions create a strong incentive for liberals to run as Republicans. Some do. One was Patrick Sweeney, elected to the Wyoming House in 2016. Sweeney is widely considered to be a real RINO, even by local journalists and allies. He winks at this by sporting a rhino pin on his lapel. Sweeney is pro-choice and votes consistently for tax increases. In the wake of George Floyd's murder, Sweeney sponsored a bill that would have required anti-bias training for police officers.[20]

---

[17] William H. Frey, "Turnout in 2020 Election Spiked Among Both Democratic and Republican Voting Groups, New Census Data Shows," *Brookings Metro Report*, May 5, 2021, https://www.brookings.edu/research/turnout-in-2020-spiked-among-both-democratic-and-republican-voting-groups-new-census-data-shows/.

[18] Stella M. Rouse et al., "Growing Tea with Subnational Roots: Tea Party Affiliation, Factionalism, and GOP Politics in State Legislatures," *American Politics Research* 50(, no. 2 (2022): 242–54.

[19] For an excellent discussion of sellouts in the context of American racial politics, see Randall Kenney, *Sellout: The Politics of Racial Betrayal* (Vintage Books, 2008).

[20] For the full text of the bill, see State of Wyoming 68th Legislature, "HB0218: Bias Motivated Crime," https://wyoleg.gov/Legislation/2021/HB0218.

Sweeney was defeated in the 2022 Republican primary, partly because of all the attention critics brought to his voting record. That outcome seems like a reasonable policing of group boundaries to us.

The larger problem in the GOP today, though, is not that genuine RINOs like Patrick Sweeney are being pushed out of the party. Instead, the problem is that they are believed to be on the march everywhere, since practically any departure from the new conservative identity politics is enough to raise suspicions. A similar problem is playing out on the left, where concepts like harm and prejudice are expanding fast, including a much broader range of behaviors.[21] The danger is that terms like "racist" and "RINO" will become utterly meaningless. If everyone is a racist or RINO, then these labels lose their coherence and even their force.

Some might still object, not unreasonably, that cancel culture is a fundamentally different threat to, say, newspapers or universities than it is to parties. After all, the former are fundamentally liberal institutions, committed to the free exchange of ideas. This is why many are especially troubled by cancel culture in universities.[22] But parties are different. They are held together by philosophical and political commitments, and thus are necessarily more tribal and parochial.

Parties, though, also can become too doctrinaire. Practically speaking, major parties can only have so many litmus tests in a two-party system like America's. As Michael Lind reminds us, usually American parties unite around a few core issues, allowing their officeholders more flexibility on others. "But by 2016," Lind observes, "the Republican party was acting more like a sect than a party. It had more articles of dogma than the Anglican Church's Thirty-Nine."[23] Lind

---

[21] See Nick Haslam, "Concept Creep: Psychology's Expanding Concepts of Harm and Pathology," *Psychological Inquiry* 27, no. 1 (2016): 1–17.

[22] As the sociologist Musa al-Gharbi lamented, "rather than serving as bastions for free exchange of ideas and the exploration of controversial topics, the state of discourse on campus seems substantially less free than that of the broader society." See Musa al-Gharbi, "Actually, Students Seem Substantially Less Free Than the General Public," *Heterodox Academy*, April 19, 2019, https://heterodoxacademy.org/blog/student-freedom-general-public/.

[23] Michael Lind, "What Politics Is(n't): In defense of What Politics Is and Is Not," *The Smart Set*, September 30, 2016, https://www.thesmartset.com/what-politics-isnt/.

doesn't exaggerate. In 2021, the Wyoming Republican Party passed 65 resolutions.[24] Liberal democracy, Lind adds, "cannot flourish with a [Republican Party] that equates ordinary political compromise with the betrayal of principle."[25]

Also, if we're going to take different types of institutions seriously— as we just did in our comparison of universities and parties—then we also need to consider the unique institutional needs of state and local governments. These institutions are built to address local needs. But, alas, the nationalization of American politics is creating a mismatch between the powers these subnational institutions actually possess and the issues they're asked to address.[26] For example, immigration is undoubtedly an important issue, but it's not one that can be sorted out by Wyoming's state legislature. And if we dump problems on institutions they can't ameliorate, we're only inviting more cynicism and distrust, further undermining their authority and thus ability to function well.

One of the biggest problems with the new identity politics more generally is that it doesn't consider the unique virtues and purposes of different institutions. Instead, it reduces them all to a stage, a place to perform and express identity. In this way of seeing things, county parties, state legislatures, and city councils are all platforms, the central difference mainly being one of size. These political institutions are thus regarded as little different from X (formerly Twitter), the favored institution of identitarians of all political persuasions. Yuval Levin has emphasized this problem, noting: "We have moved, roughly speaking, from thinking of institutions that shape people's character and habits toward seeing them as platforms that allow people to be themselves and to display themselves before a wider world." This corrupts our political institutions, Levin says, partly because treating them as platforms suffocates their "inner life—a sanctum where its work is really done."[27]

---

[24] A full list of resolutions can be found on the Wyoming Republican Party's website, https://www.wyoming.gop/blog/categories/2021-scc-resolutions.

[25] Lind, "What Politics Is(n't)."

[26] Daniel J. Hopkins, *The Increasingly United States: How and Why American Political Behavior Nationalized* (University of Chicago Press, 2018), 229.

[27] Yuval Levin, *A Time to Build: From Family and Community to Congress and the Campus, How Recommitting to Our Institutions Can Revive the American Dream* (Basic Books, 2020), 33–34, 51.

That inner world is under strain in Wyoming, all in the name of identity and transparency. One of the more poignant stories we heard during our travels was told by Stan Blake, a Democrat who served in the Wyoming House during the Bush, Obama, and Trump years. Blake had fond memories of the House's once vital inner life. After long days at work, Blake loved to join his fellow legislators—Democrats and Republicans alike—around a piano in the state capitol to sing songs together. Blake himself has a beautiful voice, and he loved leading his colleagues in "Ragtime Cowboy Joe," the fight song of the University of Wyoming. (He sang it for us with great relish.) But that unifying tradition was abruptly discontinued in the Trump years, Blake lamented. The reason, he says, is that members simply felt too exposed, especially as the new guard types used social media to publicize the inner workings of the legislature. Bipartisan frivolity might look like corruption to outsiders, such as when a picture of a Democratic and Republican lawmaker high-fiving each other was posted on Facebook, spurring nasty attacks.

And while a hostility to institutionalism is consistent with some radical or liberationist philosophies, it seems hard to square with anything resembling conservatism. Genuine conservatives, it should be remembered, have always been institutionalists. This is because they understand that institutions are necessary to direct and educate wayward human beings. Conservatives are society's proper custodians, protecting its fragile inheritance.[28] If they don't play that role, it's hard to see how conservatives can be, well, conservative. Here again, Yuval Levin makes this point well: "I don't think conservatism can do its job in a free society in opposition to the institutions of that society. I think it can only function in defense of them."[29]

That's quite an irony. Wyoming's new guard, so obsessed with recovering an authentic conservatism, is fundamentally hostile to it. In the name of conservatism, it wages war on our nation's core institutions,

---

[28] See, for example, Jerry Z. Muller, ed., *Conservatism: An Anthology of Social and Political Thought from David Hume to the Present* (Princeton University Press, 1997).

[29] See interview, Ezra Klein Show, "An Appalled Republican Considers the Future of the GOP: Yuval Levin Traces the Party's Path from Ronald Reagan to Marjorie Taylor Greene," *New York Times*, February 5, 2021, https://www.nytimes.com/2021/02/05/opinion/ezra-klein-podcast-yuval-levin.html?showTranscript=1.

sure in the conviction that none are worth preserving. Anne Applebaum made a similar observation of the populist right in Europe: "Although they hate the phrase, the new right is more Bolshevik than Burkean, these are men and women who want to overthrow, bypass, or undermine existing institutions, to destroy what exists."[30] In another turn of the screw, it is the real conservatives—those reviled as traitorous RINOs—who are the new right's enemies. Yet, Wyoming's RINOs are the ones working to preserve what is best in the state's political traditions. It is the RINOs who are the real conservatives; the identitarians are the fake ones.

---

[30] Anne Applebaum, *Twilight of Democracy: The Seductive Lure of Authoritarianism* (Anchor Books, 2021), 20.

APPENDIX

———————

Notes on Method

All told, we made five trips to Wyoming from August 2021 to July 2022, hitting the state's scattered towns, including its two largest cities (Casper and Cheyenne) and its smaller towns (Evanston, Riverton, Rock Springs, Sheridan, and Wheatland). We did not travel (alas) to Jackson in Teton County, Wyoming's most famous tourist destination. Jackson is mostly full of the second homes of the uber rich. For this reason Wyomingites barely consider it part of the state. We did one batch of interviews together to help assure that we were approaching Wyomingites in a similar way. Throughout the book, though, we use a royal "we" when presenting our findings, largely for the sake of readability.

In total, we conducted in-depth interviews with 32 individuals (see Table A.1). The interviews generally ran at least an hour, though many ran much longer, depending (in part) on our ability to establish rapport with each subject. We did not approach them with a long slate of specific questions, as a survey researcher would. Instead, our questions were more open-ended and often shifting, though all with the aim of gathering a deeper understanding of the party's factional divides. Our questions became sharper as our immersion in the state began to clarify its politics. For example, as we tuned into the importance of the urban–rural divide, we asked more questions about it in subsequent interviews. We did circle back, though, to some of our first interviewees to see what they made of the insights we had been nursing along the way.

As much as possible, we attempted to select a diverse range of individuals to interview. To a large degree, we succeeded. We interviewed elected officials, journalists, party activists, as well as Democrats and Republicans (in both the party's old and new guard). However, we had much more success securing interviews with old guard Republicans than the new insurgents, largely because the latter were almost universally suspicious of us. When we asked one typical new guard member

Table A.1 List of Interviews, 2021–2022

1. Jeremy Adler, Deputy Chief of Staff of Communications to Congresswoman Liz Cheney
2. Anonymous, Republican Party activist from Laramie County
3. Chad Banks, former Wyoming state representative, Democrat
4. Stan Blake, former Wyoming state representative, Democrat
5. John Brown, Republican Party activist from Fremont County
6. Landon Brown, Wyoming state representative, Republican
7. Cathy Connolly, Wyoming state representative, Democrat
8. Joey Correnti, Republican Party activist from Carbon County
9. Freddy Flores, Republican Party activist from Laramie County
10. Laurie Goodman, former assistant to US Senator Al Simpson
11. Robert "Matt" Grant, Republican Party activist from Natrona County
12. Elisabeth "Biffy" Jackson, Republican Party activist from Uinta County
13. Tom James, Wyoming state senator, Republican
14. Barry Jackson, Republican strategist, Washington, DC
15. Kevin Lewis, Republican Party activist from Laramie County
16. Joe McGinley, Republican Party activist from Natrona County
17. Anne MacKinnon, former editor-in-chief, *Casper Star-Tribune*
18. Jenefer Pasqua, Democratic Party activist from Laramie County
19. Nick Reynolds, journalist at WyoFile
20. Wendy Schuler, Wyoming state senator, Republican
21. Anonymous, Republican Party activist from Teton County
22. Susan Stubson, Republican Party activist from Natrona County
23. Tim Stubson, former Wyoming state representative and Republican Party activist from Natrona County
24. Patrick Sweeney, Wyoming state representative, Republican
25. Gail Symons, Republican Party activist from Sheridan County
26. Kevin Taheri, Republican Party activist from Natrona County
27. JoAnn True, donor and Republican Party activist from Natrona County
28. Isabel Wallop, Republican Party activist from Big Horn County and widow of US Senator Malcolm Wallop
29. Tom Walters, Wyoming state representative, Republican
30. Bob Wharff, Wyoming state representative, Republican
31. Sue Wilson, Wyoming state representative, Republican
32. Nathan Winters, Republican Party activist from Laramie County

for an interview, she said, sharply: "I do not talk to liberals." Little we said seemed to melt this distrust, not even mentioning our support for Republican candidates in the past. As a consequence we secured interviews with only six new guard activists and politicians: Joey Correnti, Freddy Flores, Elisabeth "Biffy" Jackson,

Tom James, Bob Wharff, and Kevin Lewis. Those half-dozen interviews were illuminating but few in number compared to the 20 interviews we did with old guard Republicans and even fewer than the seven interviews we did with journalists and Democrats.

Thus, as we digested our fieldwork, we feared that our analysis might be unduly influenced by this imbalance, a bias compounded by the deeper social and political affinities we share with establishment Republicans. We undeniably felt some real kinship with old guard Republicans, making it easy for us to develop rapport with them and sympathize with their point of view. And, of course, the book's conclusions should be read as a broader, if tempered, defense of the Republican establishment. Even so, we also (generally) liked the new guard members we spoke with. We were impressed with them at times, too. It's hard not to admire a figure like Tom James, a guy who managed to become a state senator despite the humblest of backgrounds.

More importantly, though, our research on new guard Republicans wasn't solely based on a handful of in-depth interviews. We also observed politics close up—and those observations allowed us to see many new guard Republicans we didn't interview. Our observations at the state Republican convention and at small candidate meet-and-greets, for example, allowed us to see the new party insurgents actively engaging in politics. Arguably, these observations are more revealing than long, formal interviews might have been, had we been able to secure more of them. Since we define the new right's politics as essentially performative—as one centered around the expression and affirmation of an authentic conservatism—there is no substitute for these observations.

And while we were only able to get a handful of in-depth interviews with new guard Republicans, we did manage to secure shorter, more casual conversations with members of their rank and file as well as some of their most important leaders, including Marti Halverson and even the party's state chair Frank Eathorne. Those encounters, brief as they were, still provided us with a richer sense of their world. We also combed through many written party materials, including resolutions and platforms.

The irony, here, is that these new guard Republicans are hardly shy in public life. After all, the nature of their politics—which typically involves expressing their opinions in open, strident ways—tends to attract media attention. Our research benefited greatly from the diligent work of local journalists in Wyoming, many of whom have followed these factional disputes long before we showed up in the summer of 2021. We often leaned on their work and interviews with them to better understand the state's Republican politics and round out our research.

Scattered sources of evidence, mostly from journalists, suggest that our account of the Republican civil war holds beyond the small state of Wyoming. But verifying this impression will, of course, depend on other deep dives into state and local politics beyond the Cowboy state. We hope more work—by both journalists and social scientists—is done to provide a fuller account of the current struggle over the Republican Party.

ACKNOWLEDGMENTS

We are indebted to many colleagues and friends. We are especially grateful to George Thomas, the director of Claremont McKenna's Salvatori Center, for generously funding our fieldwork. Additionally, we are grateful to our friends and colleagues at Claremont McKenna College for creating such an ideal intellectual environment to research and write. In Wyoming, many went out of their way to help us, particularly Landon Brown, Nick Reynolds, Tim Stubson, and Susan Stubson. This work would be impossible without their help. At Oxford University Press, we owe a great debt to Dave McBride, who skillfully and patiently navigated the manuscript through the review process. Morgan Jones provided valuable editorial feedback, greatly improving the cogency of our manuscript. Andrew Pachuta skillfully copy-edited our manuscript and Abishayareddy Vijaybabu expertly managed its production. We are also indebted to three reviewers. Their feedback improved our work considerably. Finally, Steve Teles at Johns Hopkins University supported this project in countless ways.

This book is dedicated to our mentors, Peter Skerry and Brian Balogh. They are both model teachers and scholars, exemplifying intellectual virtues we always aim to emulate, however much we fall short. We are forever in their debt.

INDEX

For the benefit of digital users, indexed terms that span two pages (e.g., 52–53) may, on occasion, appear on only one of those pages.